A Tale Teller's Tale

Richard G. Constable

First published in Great Britain in 2019

This first edition published in 2019 by
Lapwing Publishing Services
2 Siren Cottages, Horsgate Lane, Cuckfield RH17 5AZ

http://www.lapwingpublishing.com

British Library Cataloguing-in-Publication Data
A catalogue record for this book is available from the British Library

ISBN   978-1-9993226-1-8

Printed and bound by Ashford Colour Press, UK

This book is dedicated to my Aunt Clara to whom I owe so much.

Preface

Textthis story of my life is written almost completely from memory and is not intended to be a totally accurate account of the truth. Some of the events may quite well be remembered differently by others as very few, if any, records are kept of the incidents that are described.

I was born on October 14th 1943 during the Second World War, from when memories started to accumulate in my mind. I was the fourth son born to John William Constable and Mildred Constable (née Taylor), both very much from a working-class background. John (Jack) Constable was a bricklayer as were his father, grandfather and great grandfather. Mildred (Millie) was a laundry girl and spent her whole life associated with that industry, in one form or another.

This account of life in the second half of the twentieth century has been written for family and friends and not intended for general reading but, if it interests others, then so much the better.

Richard Constable

Cuckfield, West Sussex

Acknowledgements

My thanks to Jennifer, my wife, and children, Emma and Mathew, for the tremendous support and encouragement to write this account of my life. They really had to push me. To their forbearance in listening to my stories so many times over the years and without showing the slightest sense of boredom or impatience.

Finally, an enormous thank you to Gavin Jamieson, my independent Publisher and Consultant, who without his patience, guidance and understanding, I would have abandoned all hope of achieving my task to finish the whole process.

Contents

Contents *(continued)*

Chapter 1
Grandparents

As strange as it may seem I think my life began long before I was born and now I have reached later years it also seems to have been planned throughout.

It all began in about 1900 when my grandmother, Dad's mother, Nan Alice, arrived in my home town of Brighton. Nan was a farm workers daughter in a small hamlet called Upton in Norfolk, England, whose mother Mary Reed (née Mary George) had died when she was only eleven years old. Her father William Reed married again soon after but her new stepmother didn't like her, and she suffered beatings and general abuse. Nan made the decision that as soon as she was old enough and was able to accumulate enough money she would escape from the life that was making her so unhappy. As part of her plan and as soon as she was able to get away from school she obtained a position as a housemaid in a large house at 12 Thorpe Road, just up the road from Norwich railway station. This I would suspect was to allow her a quick getaway when the time was right. When the big day arrived, she gathered her few belongings together and readied herself to make a run for it, she told nobody of what she was about to do so that she would just disappear never to be seen again by her family and friends.

Nan had never been outside of Norfolk before and had never even been on a train, but she had planned her escape well and was adamant that she would never return. Once she had obtained her ticket and was on the train she sat by the window in the third-class carriage and soon came to terms with what

The earliest photograph of my Nan Constable.

My grandparents, Alfred and Alice Constable outside Number 9, Baxter Street.

she had done and concluded that there was no turning back. What was done was done.

On arrival at Kings Cross station, Nan's plan of escape was to cross London to Victoria station. She had read in a magazine that this was the departure point for many holiday resorts on the south coast and, consequently, this was where she thought she may be able to obtain employment. Once at Victoria the big decision had to be made of where to go and what train to get. In the end the decision was made for her as it was starting to get quite late in the day and she had no idea what she would find at her destination, or where she would sleep that night.

Only one train was scheduled to leave in the next half hour and that was to Brighton, a place she knew little about. However, she decided to take this train as the map showed Brighton as the end of the line and therefore was probably a seaside resort. After buying her ticket at the kiosk she made her way to the platform where the ticket collector in his smart uniform was busy clipping tickets. Nan never told us what happened after she arrived in Brighton only that she got a job in a large house as a maid and went on to meet my grandfather.

My grandfather, Alfred John Henry Constable, was as they say a complete different 'kettle of fish' from my Nan. Very few people liked him, including me, and on reflection I don't think he even liked himself. His family were from Mid-Sussex but his parents, Alfred Henry Constable and Clara Ann Constable (née Standen), were born in Mid-Sussex but married in Brighton. Grandad's great grandparents died in the workhouse for destitute people in Cuckfield (more of that later in the story of how I made this discovery). Grandad's parents moved to Brighton searching for work in the middle of the 19th century, later moving to 7 Cromwell Street, Brighton, off of Elm Grove, where grandad was born. There are several versions of grandad's life but the family in general, and my grandfather in particular, could in my mum's words "tell a good tale", in other words lie through his teeth. One tale he used to tell us children was when he was a boy he used to dive for pennies off of the Palace Pier, thrown by visitors over the side for him and others to retrieve. I think this may have an element of truth in it but the only contact with water that I ever knew he had was a bath once a week like the rest of us or getting it down his throat in the form of pints of beer. Grandad was a bricklayer and said he was in the Royal Horse Artillery. It has since come to light that he was nothing of the sort and was only a reserve private soldier. That's not to say that he was definitely not in the Royal Horse Artillery, it's just not recorded in any official records that I have looked at. My brother Terence provided me with Grandad's army identity card showing he was a member of No. 10 Kent and Sussex 2nd Armoured Division and his army number was 374245 – which makes no reference to the Royal Horse Artillery – but, to repeat my mum, "he could tell a good tale".

How my Nan met Grandad is a mystery, but it never seemed to be a match made in heaven. Perhaps it was in the beginning, but he was a violent man especially when he had been drinking, which was quite often. Nan would often suffer from physical abuse from Grandad. Of course, in those days there wasn't anywhere else to run to, particularly for Nan who had no contact with her family.

Nan and Grandad were married at Preston Old Church on January 20th 1906 and started married life at Number 11, Herbert Street, Brighton. Their first born was a boy by the name of William John Constable (my Dad, and always known as Jack) although Grandad's name was Alfred he was always known as Jack at work, but Alf to Nan. One day when Grandad had again been treating Nan badly, my Dad who was home on leave from the army and idolised his mum, decided enough was enough. Nan was crying and in pain from a beating dished out by Grandad, Dad insisted on being told what had happened. As soon as he saw the results of what Grandad had done he went for him, held him up against the wall and threatened him with his very large fist and told him that that was what he should expect if he ever touched his mother again. Needless to say, he never did, but he did cause her heartache in other ways. One thing that comes to mind was when Grandad tried to commit suicide. He did this by slitting his throat in the outside toilet, Nan found him in a pool of blood wedged behind the door and couldn't get at him. When they eventually got him out he was nearly gone but was saved and sewn back together. I remember the unusual crease under his neck where the stitching together took place. I am pretty sure I remember when he did it so it probably all took place in the late 1940s or early 1950s.

To help Nan augment the family income and to try to make ends meet she took several jobs, one being as a cloakroom attendant at the Brighton Aquarium Dance Hall. Her wages were not over generous but that did not deter my Nan as she worked out how to increase this by putting two coats on one hanger for each couple and issuing one numbered ticket but charging for two, thereby making a handsome profit at the end of the evening.

Grandad spent most of the household income on alcohol so Nan was always short of money and had to try to stretch what she did get to make ends meet but of course she never could. To help her through the week she would have to take the sheets off of the beds and wash them before taking them to the pawnbrokers along with Grandad's best suit (this was only worn on Sundays when Grandad went to the pub). Anything of value would be taken in on Monday morning and redeemed on Friday after Grandad had been paid on Thursday. I don't know what would have happened if he failed to provide sufficient money to get the goods back. Pawn shops were places that you could get short term loans on which you had to pay an interest payment in return for depositing your goods as security. If you failed to redeem your goods within a specified period then you forfeited the goods and the pawnbroker was able to sell them without any compensation.

Nan was never happier then when she was visiting us in our little house at 9 Baxter Street, Brighton. She was able to visit often as Nan and Grandad lived at 25 Pankhurst Avenue, just a short walk along Queens Park Road. She would make any excuse to call in to our house, but we were not allowed to let Grandad know she was there or had visited as he would always complain if he found out where she had been. Grandad always had to be the centre of attention.

Another one of Nan's small pleasures was horse racing and as she lived close to Brighton racecourse she would take my brothers and I out for the afternoon to watch and play in the mounds of hay at the end of the course run off. Her favourite horses were those which had the name red included in their name, for example Red Alligator, Red Light etc. Nan could not afford to bet but occasionally would put a sixpenny piece on a 'Red' horse and would very often win.

After the Second World War, and in the 1950s, Nan and Grandad would come to lunch with us on Sundays when I always sat next to her to hold her hand and smell her special smell. I am sitting here now in my mid-70s and can still smell her special aroma and feel her close by.

It was at this time that a strange thing quite often happened to me at Sunday lunch and I have no idea why or how it happened. I would be sitting eating my lunch (we always called it dinner then in our ignorance). I would start to float out of my seat and levitate above the table and would be looking down at the rest of the family. Nobody ever noticed what was happening and no comment was ever made so I can only surmise that it was either a mental or physical problem relating to my growing so fast. To this day I have no idea how or what caused it to happen.

Sunday afternoons following lunch was a problem for Nan as Grandad would be trying to get her to go home with him so that he could have his afternoon sleep. We children would be encouraging her in the opposite direction to stay with us and on many occasions we would succeed much to Grandad's annoyance. Our aim was to get them to stay until five pm so that mum would insist that Nan should stay to tea with us. My Mum would always make sure that Nan went home with something, normally what was left over from lunch time.

When on the odd occasion we visited my grandparent's house in Pankhurst Avenue, Grandad would never allow us children into any part of the house except the kitchen. He hated us going there and I can only remember one occasion being able to look into the main lounge and that was when Grandad was not at home, thank goodness the toilet was outside the house. Nan was a wonderful cook with many delicious recipes but our favourite was her apple tart; the thought of it still makes my mouth water. If Grandad had known we were being given apple tart and custard all hell would have broken loose.

When my maternal grandmother, Nanny Taylor died, in her 60s, my Mum and Dad had not been married very long. My Nan Constable went to my mum and said how very sorry she was and made her a promise that she would not try to replace her mother but would do her best to be her mother in every way she could. She kept that promise until the day she died.

One day Nan was going through the runners and riders of the next horse race meeting at Brighton in her favourite newspaper the Daily Mirror when she noticed a headline in a section called 'Live Letter's'. Someone was looking for his long-lost sister. Nan's eye was taken by this and she soon found herself reading part of her life story. It was her brother trying to find her. Nan didn't say anything to Grandad as he would only have tried to be difficult and would be against her making any contact, so she put her coat on and said she was going shopping and headed straight for our house. Mum and Nan were very close and both loved each other, probably more than if they were real mother and daughter. Nan was so excited when she saw Mum and wasn't sure if to laugh or cry explaining at the same time what she had discovered. The interesting thing is, that it was the first time any of us had ever heard the true story of what had happened to Nan and where she came from. Mum immediately offered to write to the editor of the Daily Mirror to see if she could obtain an address in order to make contact on Nan's behalf. After a few weeks of letters passing backwards and forwards details arrived. It was Nan's brother and he was longing to know where she was and what had happened to her.

Soon after the details arrived tragedy struck. Nan was diagnosed with cancer of the throat, which was hardly surprising as she always smoked 'Woodbine' cigarettes – the strongest and most tar-filled type you could buy. She and we children were not told it was cancer, instead we were told it was a thyroid problem. She had two operations to try to save her. She put up a brave fight but died on May 2nd 1958 at 71-years-old. As a child I just could not comprehend my lovely Nan would not be around. Oh, how we all missed her. I still do. That smell, her laugh and her love for us kids. Years later when I was old enough to drive I decided with my mum that we would travel to Norfolk to find Nan's family, and off we set with my Dad and sister Margaret. We arrived at the outskirts of the city with the address but no idea where to find it. After asking several people for directions, without success, we came upon a chemist shop with the same maiden name as Nan's, 'Reed', written above the shop front. In went my Mum and was soon back with a smile all over her face. It turned out to be one of many chemist's shops owned by one of Nan's nephews that she had never known. Off we went again following the directions we had been given and soon arrived at a very large bungalow sitting in its own grounds. We were very impressed. Out we all got and marched up to the door, rang the bell and waited. Soon after, around the corner, walked my Nan in men's clothing.

From left to right: Alfred John Constable, Martha Taylor, William Thomas Taylor, Alice Ruth Constable.

We were all so surprised, it was Nan's brother. After meeting his wife and other members of the family and relaying what had happened to Nan since she had run away, drinking lots of tea and eating cake, it was time to leave but not before being encouraged to pick bags of pears from the orchard to take with us. I am so pleased and proud that we made that journey to meet Nan's family and to fulfil Nan's desire to be reunited with her family. The only sad thing was that she could not be with us, but I'm not completely convinced of that!

Just before she died Nan had a conversation with Mum about Grandad, what would happen to him etc. Why she cared so for a man that had made her life so unhappy I have no idea, except that Nan always looked after Grandad even though he was a complete horror. As I have said before my Mum would have done anything for her mother-in-law and to the dismay of us children we were told that Grandad was coming to live with us. Mum had promised Nan that she would take care of Grandad and she never went back on her word, ever. Grandad was to be given the bedroom at the top of our stairs, known to us as the 'Slip Room', and only used by us as a store room and somewhere to put anything that we didn't know where else to put it. It seemed strange to me that this room was never used as a bedroom, especially as we were very short of space, but it all came out when we moved sometime later (I don't think Grandad was ever told, which was just as well). Mum told us that the people who lived in our house before us had a young son who was involved in a serious traffic accident in the main road at the bottom of our street. He was bought home to the house in a very serious condition and put on his bed in the small bedroom where he unfortunately died. When Mum and Dad moved into the house she said she was woken night after night by the sound of a child crying and calling out in pain coming from the Slip Room. I just remember whenever I ventured into the room it felt very cold and made the hairs on my neck rise, but I didn't know why at the time, thank goodness.

Nan and Grandad Constable had several children: William John (Jack, my Dad), Charlie, Sydney, Ernie, Harry and a daughter named Queenie who I never met as she fell out with my Nan. I don't know why but let me just say as wonderful as we thought our Nan was you wouldn't want to get on the wrong side of her, not even her daughter. We never knew anything about Grandad Constable's family as he never told us but many years later I found out quite a lot by pure coincidence. He was born in Brighton, at Number 7 Cromwell Street, and went on to become a bricklayer, one of many in the construction industry before and since, was all we knew. His mother died when he was a child but he never spoke of that to anyone. We did know that he had a half-brother by the name of Harry, we only knew that as I remember him coming to see Grandad after Nan died. Grandad had a few stories that I can remember and one was that he helped out on a milk round when he was a boy and used to go to the Queen's Park to water down the milk to make it go around further. Like most of Grandad's family you never knew what was true or not but I suspect it was true, anything was possible in those very austere times. Grandad died on January 8th 1962, at our new house (Number 96, Havelock Road) that we had moved to in order to accomodate him. He simply went to bed one evening and never woke up, no suffering, no pain, he just simply faded away, I still wonder where the justice was in that. I remember the night as I had been in bed for several days with a serious bought of flu which was raging in the population at the time. I woke and could hear weird noises coming from downstairs, a sort of wailing and croaking (we had moved house by then and Grandad had a room downstairs). I'm not sure if it was Grandad breathing his last but that's what I thought in the morning when Mum found him and told me what had happened. I was about 14-years-old at the time and of course it could all be my imagination, but I also remember the undertakers coming to collect him and all the noises that went with that, so I am convinced what I remember is fact. One other strange thing occurred that seems to confirm my story. My Mum told me that the clock in Grandad's room stopped in the early hours of the morning which was the time that I was lying awake listening to the noise coming from downstairs. I have always thought this a bit spooky and strange but that's what happened.

My Mum's parents were very different from my Constable grandparents. Grandad was Arthur John Taylor and my grandmother was Martha Taylor (née Washington). Their parents were Arthur John Taylor and Sarah Ann Taylor (née Miles) from Epsom in Surrey. Grandad and his brother married my Nanny Taylor and my Nanny's sister. This marriage caused me much confusion when I was a child because their offspring looked so much alike and resembled my mum in particular. Even as a teenager I would often mistake my Mum's cousins for her, especially when shopping in the London Road. I would approach them only to suddenly realise that it wasn't my Mum. They always smiled at me and seemed to understand, and I am sure it helped

Nan Taylor, a mother – it is said – to 21 children.

that I looked like my mum myself. Other family members probably approached my Mum in the same way.

My Nanny Taylor was born on September 25th 1876 at 43 Egremont Street, Brighton, and died at the age of 61 years on June 8th 1938 at 70 Warleigh Road, Brighton, before I was born. Her photographs show her as rather a large lady with a big round face and she looked a real handful. Dying at such a young age is not surprising when you consider that it is said she had 21 children. There has always been a doubt as to the exact number she had as quite a few died either at childbirth or at a young age. I did seem to have numerous aunts and uncles, many of them I liked very much but some seemed a bit strange to me. This may be because many on Mum's side of the family suffered with mental difficulties.

My Grandad, William Thomas Taylor.

Nanny Taylor was a staunch member of the Salvation Army, based in the Congress Hall opposite the 'Level' recreation ground in the centre of Brighton. This had once been the Sussex County Cricket Ground in a former life. Because of this, her house was always full of waifs and strays from society as she never turned anyone away who was in need. Some stopped for days and a few became regular members of her and Grandad's extended family. How she managed to find the resources and money to feed such numbers remains a mystery. Grandad had a large allotment and mum said that she remembered that most of the produce was used to feed the extended family, other than that we were never told.

One of Mum's sisters, Aunt Daisy, got pregnant before she was married (something that in those days was considered outrageous in a society where you became an outcast in such circumstances). One thing that sticks in my mind is that everyone in the family referred to the father of the child as being 'handsome, tall and dishy'. I think quite a few of my aunts were a bit jealous. It was decided that the pregnancy was to be kept a secret in the family as the young man in question decided to do a bunk, never to be seen again. My Aunt insisted she was going to keep the baby and bring it up herself, not that she had much choice as my Grandmother made all the decisions in her house and was too religious to allow anything else to happen. Everything went well at the birth of a little boy who was named Leslie Taylor. A short time after, Nanny Taylor heard a crash on the floor in the room where Aunt Daisy was recovering from the birth. She flew up the stairs to see what had happened only to find my Aunt fast asleep and the baby screaming its head off lying on the floor. Scooping up the baby and waking my aunt at the same time she told my aunt that she was unfit to bring up a child and that, from then on, the boy would be brought up as her younger brother and that was that, no arguments.

I was over the age of 40 before I was told that my Uncle Les was in fact my cousin. The secret had been kept by the whole family, and nobody outside my grandparents' house ever knew, such was the stigma. My Aunt Daisy didn't learn much from her first mistake and it wasn't long before she was pregnant by someone else and gave birth to another boy who was called Ronnie. I only knew him as Ronnie Falger, the surname of the man who Aunt Daisy eventually married.

Mum decided to check on Daisy one day when Ron was about 5-years-old, as she was struggling to cope. When Mum got to her flat in Upper Lewes Road she knocked on the communal front door but got no reply and, as the door was slightly open, she went in and climbed the stairs to Daisy's entrance door. There was an awful commotion going on inside, so in Mum went to find poor Ronnie stark naked cowering under the dining table with Aunt Daisy beating him with a leather belt. Mum could see the red marks all over Ron's body who was screaming for his life. Shouting at Aunt Daisy to stop, she grabbed the belt from her and rescued Ronnie from under the table. Mum never told me what happened next only that Ronnie came to stay with us where he recovered from his ordeal. After this episode nothing like it happened again, probably because my Mum took a very close interest in cousin Ronnie's welfare and Aunt Daisy knew not to cross my Mum. Ronnie suffered for the rest of his life from his terrible childhood where he didn't receive any love except from my mum and our family.

When Ron grew up he met a girl who he believed cared for him and he became devoted to her. Mum encouraged the relationship by getting them both to visit us where she let them use our front room to be together for the odd evening. Happiness was not something Ronnie was used to and of course it never lasted; it all came tumbling down when he found out that the girl was seeing someone else. He was beside himself and came to Mum in the hope that she could rescue his situation but of course there was little she could do. It was at this point that Ronnie decided to take matters into his own hands. After obtaining a large kitchen knife he lay in wait for the girl in a side street off the Lewes Road. When she turned the corner, he pounced on her and tried to kill her only to be thwarted by some men who were passing by. After he was disarmed, and the police were called, he was arrested on the charge of attempted murder. Following his trial, which Mum attended, he was sentenced to 10 years in jail.

All through the long years that Ronnie was incarcerated Mum visited him as often as she could. She could ill afford the fares to the prisons, money was something we didn't have much of, but Mum was not prepared to abandon him. When he was eventually released he disappeared completely and made no contact with anyone, including Mum, and she was so upset. Years later contact was made with Mum by a lady who was the landlady of a pub in east London who went on to explain what had happened to Ronnie since his release from

Back row: Mum, Dad, Nan Constable; Front row: Jack, Terence, Margaret, Richard, Brian (circa 1950).

jail. It was Ronnie's wife who had convinced him to make contact with his family, which he agreed to, on the condition that the only one he wanted to know was my Mum. Time passed, and Ron's wife and Mum encouraged him to visit us before, in his early 50s, he suddenly died of heart failure all brought about, I am sure, by his sad, sad life.

The day my Nanny Taylor died she was in good spirits but started to get very tired and decided to go to bed for a lie down. Shortly before going up the stairs she said to one of her daughters "would you like a bite of my banana?". "Yes please" said my aunt. "Well, you can't", came the reply and off she went bed. That was the last words she ever spoke and the last that she was seen alive. She just laid on her bed and died with the banana still in her hand. My eldest brother Jack was the only one of us children that she knew in our family, and only then as a baby. I have always wished I had known her.

Grandad Taylor and his family came from Epsom in Surrey and was born on September 24th 1876, married Nanny Taylor on April 4th 1899, and died on August 13th 1957. Records show that Grandad lived at 34 Picton Street, and Nanny lived at Number 38, so I presume that is how they met.

At the outset of the First World War in 1914, Grandad was despatched to France and it was here that his life was changed for ever, as many young lives were. Being gassed in the trenches was not uncommon and Grandad became a casualty of this barbaric act of the German enemy. He suffered for the rest of his life with fits and other difficulties but managed to survive until the age of 81. Fortunately, he was very careful with money or, as Mum would say, 'tight as a drum'.

Grandad did however manage to accumulate money by loaning it out to friends and family at an interest rate acceptable to both. Mum said that he kept all the details in a large ledger book which he always kept hidden away together with the details and membership of what was known as a 'Tontine' club. This was a sort of savings club for members of the family and others. They would pay in a regular sum of money each week and were paid out depending on the order they were drawn out of a hat. I am not absolutely sure exactly how the rules worked but that was the gist of it. Interest on the money from the operation was paid to the members but grandad would have taken his cut I'm sure.

Mum always insisted that I was an image of her father, not only his fair skin and red hair but his ways as well. I think she was right. The idea of making money has always been a strong point of mine.

Mum used to tell us the story (as she did many times) of when, on a rare occasion, she was travelling back to our house with him and he suggested that they caught a bus. We never travelled by bus normally and walked everywhere to save money and Mum said she had little money in her purse for the rest of the week and thought that Grandad was going to pay. When the bus conductor came to collect the fares he just sat there with his arms folded and simply ignored him. Poor Mum was so embarrassed she had to turn out her purse and just managed to scrape enough together to pay the fares. It cleaned her out for the week.

It's fair to say that Mum never got on with her father. She liked life and wanted to live it to the full and when she was young did her best to do just that. One evening she was all dressed up and had her makeup on with the latest in hair and dress design. Mum was a very attractive girl and just wanted to enjoy herself, but Grandad was very much the puritan and found such behaviour much against his beliefs and wishes. She saw Grandad walking towards her up the road, and crossed over in an attempt to avoid him, but when she crossed he went over. She kept her head down to hide the dreaded makeup. When at last they got close enough, Grandad went right up to mum and looked her straight in the eye and uttered the following, never forgotten, verdict: "You think you look really beautiful with that stuff on, but you don't, you look as ugly as pig sh**t" and walked straight past her.

I think this is probably why we were kept at a distance from him and without my Grandmother, who Mum loved, there was no one to keep the peace between them.

Chapter 2
My Arrival

I was born on the October 14th 1943 at the height of the Second World War and was the youngest of four boys: John (Jack), Brian, Terence and me. There were good things about being the youngest child, not least with being the centre of everyone's attention. I enjoyed that for three years plus, until my sister Margaret came along and ruined it for me on May 6th 1947. Oh, what a shock that was to find she was getting all the attention that should have been lavished on me! I refused to walk, stopped eating (not for long) and made such a fuss. However, it was no good. My day in the sun had passed, but I wasn't happy and made sure everyone knew. I even cornered my Aunt Clara one day and made her promise that she still loved me. I've never accepted second best at anything since.

Me as a baby in the arms of Jack. Brian is on the left, and Terence on the right.

I'm getting ahead of my story. I was delivered into this world in the top front bedroom of our house at 9 Baxter Street, Brighton. It had two bedrooms and what was known as the slip room at the top of the stairs. On the ground floor was what we called the front room (lounge) which we were only allowed to use on special occasions, Christmas and Friday night singing practice with Mr Pollard our church organist and choir master. In the middle was a room we called the kitchen, it wasn't, it was the dining room where we all ate our meals together. And at the back was the scullery where the backdoor was, which it also wasn't, it was the kitchen where all the cooking, washing and bath night took place. Out the back door and across a small yard were the steps leading to the outside toilet.

Dad very rarely carried out any decorations to our house, so it was always a bit shabby; spotlessly clean, but shabby. Mum did on one occasion convince Dad to wallpaper our hall which he did with a lovely light printed pattern. All went well and was completed over one weekend which transformed the hall into a nice light space. On the Tuesday, every two weeks, the coal man would deliver to our street and we were on the list for the next delivery which happened to coincide with the completion of Dad's hard work. Now, in a small terrace house, the only place to store coal was under the stairs, the door to which was in the newly decorated hall. Up the steps the coal man came and into the house with the sack of coal on his back, along the hall where he had to turn a sharp left turn to tip the coal into the cupboard. As he carried out this tricky move he dragged the corner of the sooty sack all along the new wallpaper leaving a thick black mark which couldn't be removed. My Dad, to my knowledge, never did any more decorating that I can remember, I was just pleased not to be around when he got home.

Three houses away at Number 3 lived the lady who was to become the most influential person in my life other than my wife. I hesitate to write this as I loved Mum and Nan Constable, but this lady was the one that taught me so much about everything, including myself, and set me up for everything I have achieved in my life.

Mrs Clara Bentick was her name, a widow due to a tragic accident during the construction of the stone entrance pylons on the London to Brighton Road [A23] on the outskirts of Brighton. Her husband's name was William Bentick and was to become known to me as Uncle Will, even though I never met him and was not related to him.

Before I was born, and Mum pregnant, she got talking to Mrs Bentick in the street outside her house, as people did in those times. Mum was saying how difficult it was going to be for her with already having three young boys and that she had no idea how she would cope when I turned up. "Don't you worry my dear" said Mrs Bentick, "just give me a shout and I will help in any way I can".

Neither Mum, or this lady from down the road, thought much more about it until I started to arrive. The mid-wife had been called but had yet to turn up. I was arriving fast and Mum needed help, when she thought of the offer made by Mrs Bentick. One of my brothers was sent to Number 3 to summon help. Mrs Bentick dropped everything and came straight away and was soon in our top front bedroom.

A studio portrait of Aunt Clara and myself.

Mrs Bentick was there helping at my birth when the mid-wife arrived and stayed to see me come into the world. After Mum, she was the first to hold me in her arms. Once everything was cleared up the mid-wife asked if the lady could keep an eye on Mum until Dad got home, which she did. It was at this point that Mum became upset and started to cry. Mrs Bentick asked what the matter was as the baby had arrived safely and all was well. Mum explained that she was dreading being left with all the children to look after and that it was a struggle as it was another mouth to feed. Mrs Bentick responded by saying she would help with looking after the children and, pointing to me, this one in particular. With that Mum handed me over to the woman who was to help bring me up, my guiding light, my teacher, my everything a child could want, known to me from then on as my Aunt Clara. Aunt Clara looked after me and when my Christening came around Mum asked my aunt if she would be my godmother. She didn't want asking twice and readily accepted. From then on Aunt Clara became my second mother.

Next was what I was to be called. My first name was given to me by my Mum, who told me once that she wanted me big and strong like a lion, Richard Coeur de Lion, and then said, "look what I got". I was very thin and weak as a child. She was never one to think before she spoke or indeed let you get above your station.

George Bentick who was killed in the Second World War. I was given the middle name of George in his memory.

My second name was given to me by Aunt Clara, as she had had an adopted son by the name of George Bentick. George had been killed in the Second World War during the battle for Crete. It was understood he made it to one of the ships helping to evacuate the troops but it was bombed by the Germans and it was assumed he went down with the ship. Many of his personal belongings surfaced years later when I was about 8-years-old, including identification papers which had been found in the attic of a sailor in Portsmouth. He had died, and his relatives had sent them on when they were found. I remember going with my Aunt to an interview in the council offices in the Royal York Buildings in Brighton where she was able to put questions to a war office representative in order to see if it could be discovered what had happened to George. I just remember how upset my Aunt was at the whole process and the mystery that was never resolved. She still believed that he was alive suffering from memory loss, she just could not accept that he was gone. So, I became Richard George after my Aunt's son, a name I have always been proud to have and to carry on in his remembrance. I loved my Aunt then and all these years later I love her still, but I do have regrets that I didn't do more for her when I became older, but she never complained.

As I grew up I spent more and more time in Aunt Clara's company. Mum often reminded me that I used to dive out of our front door and the last she would see of me was my red hair disappearing into 3 Baxter Street. We were always making things. Christmas decorations were a speciality; cooking, decorating, gardening, nothing seemed to be out of bounds for my aunt. I was allowed to have a go at anything. She taught me to knit, sew, repair anything. I can still do all these things which have been an asset to me over the years and set me up for my working life later on. When my first grandchild Leo was born I knitted his first blanket. From about 5-years-old, maybe before, we would decorate different rooms in her house and I can still smell the buckets of distemper (the predecessor of emulsion) which was made from a white powder and mixed with water to a thick goo. I was allowed to do all this without any interference. Goodness knows what mess I made, but I always got encouragement to have a go and keep going. Life for me with my Aunt Clara was just heaven

At the end of the war in 1945 things were very difficult with food, clothing and almost everything on ration. This didn't affect me very much, I was completely spoiled by my Aunt. Many meals, except Sundays, were taken with my Aunt. Just the two of us, sardines on toast, roes on toast, herrings which could be got for twelve for a shilling, you name it, if it was available, we had it. I even had a fruit cake baked especially for me every week so that when I called

My disappointment at not obtaining the yellow jumper.

in after school I could help myself to a large slice. I don't think this made me very popular with my siblings, but it certainly didn't worry me.

All my Aunt's cooking was carried out on what was known as a 'Kitchen Range', this was a wood and coal fired basket which heated the adjacent oven and hot plates. Whilst very much Victorian in design it kept the whole house warm and cooked for free at the same time. I remember sitting in my chair by the range and falling fast asleep, never to be disturbed until I woke up naturally, who was spoilt?

We were walking down Elm Grove one day when I spotted a bright canary yellow jumper in a second-hand clothes shop. Getting new clothes was almost impossible and out of reach for us because of cost. I asked my Aunt if I could have it. Why I liked it so much I don't know but want it I did. On looking closer in the window the answer I got was no and that it was too expensive at two shillings and sixpence (12.5p). I so wanted it and immediately went into a strop. We were on our way to have my photograph taken at a studio in Western Road, a very special and expensive treat for my birthday, I still have the photograph with my sour face looking back at me. Whenever I look at it, which isn't very often as it reminds me of just how spoilt I was, it is something I am not very proud of. Like most things in my life I have normally finished up with what I have wanted and, yes, I finished up with the yellow jumper when my Aunt took me back a few days later. It didn't even fit properly, was far too big but I had got my own way and was happy. What a dick, I mean Richard.

At the age of about 6 I got myself in serious trouble when walking home from school at lunch time and it was pouring with rain and puddles of water were everywhere. I decided to play jumping up and down in as many as I could in just my school shoes. Getting as far as Aunt Clara's I decided to go in and get dried out before my Mum caught me; she would not have been pleased seeing my saturated socks and shoes. Thinking she was saving me from trouble she quickly removed my wet things and dried them on her kitchen range. When they were more or less dry she put them back on again and off I went. I said nothing to Mum and she didn't question where I had been.

After a few days I started to run a temperature when Mum called in Dr Thwaites our doctor (they came to you in those days). I was soon diagnosed with a kidney complaint called 'nephritis', a problem brought on by the puddle episode, dry socks but damp shoes. I was taken into The Royal Alexandra Hospital for Sick Children, where I stayed for 3 months. I was very ill and Mum was told it could be fatal. Aunt Clara was beside herself as she said she was responsible, but how was she supposed to know.

The thing that I remember most about being in hospital was the sweet box which was taken around daily; all sweets delivered by visitors were supposed to be put in the collective box. My aunt used to bring in two bags, one for the box and one for the back of my locker. All sweets stayed on ration until 1953 so I don't know how she managed to get so many, I suppose it was just her rations?

Birthdays were a mixture of good and bad for me and my Aunt. On the one hand I had a day off school and on the other I always seemed to have to go to the school dentist, where not much advancement had been made in this form of torture. We had our teeth inspected under the new National Health Service at school, and this was at a time when fluoride in drinking water and effective toothpaste was years away, for most of the population anyway. Fillings were quite normal for children and the method of carrying this out was barbaric. On arriving at the dentist, which was housed in a beautiful but half derelict building in Carlton Hill next to the art school, you were called into the surgery to be confronted by this enormously large German lady dentist. I was always terrified. This woman had hands like an enormous bunch of bananas, one finger could hardly fit into my mouth. To have the tooth filled we were put to sleep by having a metal cage held over our open mouths, and then having a cloth put over your face and liquid dripped onto it, and by this method we fell asleep. Awful, just awful. Going to the dentist is still a bit of a trial for me which, I'm sure, relates back to those birthday visits as a boy.

Once out of the dentist off we used to go for a lovely day out which included eating lots of sugary cake, sweets and everything I shouldn't have to avoid until the following year's visit to the dentist.

Aunt Clara and I spent many hours enjoying ourselves. One way was to go to Brighton seafront and play our trick of trying to get a cheap trip on one of the charabancs (coaches) all lined up on Madeira Drive and went by the title of 'mystery trips'. Aunt Clara had a friend who drove a charabanc for a firm called 'Unique'. His name was Henry and was a short dapper man dressed in a smart suit, tie and very highly polished leather shoes. Our tactic was to walk along and get as close to Henry as we could at which time he would be asked the all-important question "Hello Henry, are you full up for your trip?". More often than not he would say no but that he still had plenty of time to get more customers. My Aunt would engage Henry in conversation for a while to put him off trying to fill his seats and to waste as much time as possible. Once we had spun it out as long as possible off we would go, returning a few minutes before the tour was to begin. This was the moment of truth, "Hello again Henry, did you manage to fill her up?". My Aunt knew full well that he hadn't sold all the seats, as she always checked it out before from the position we had been spying from on the opposite side of the road. It worked almost every time and after short negotiations it was settled at half price for Aunt Clara, and I went free but only on the condition that in Henry's words, "If I get another passenger the boy will have to sit on your lap". I never did.

Our other love was to go to the Brighton theatres of which there were many, including the Theatre Royal, The Dome, and the Hippodrome where in 1953/54 I saw the famous comedy act of Laurel and Hardy. 'Tuesday Night at The Dome' was wonderful when, at the end of all the acts, my Aunt and I would join with the rest of the audience in singing our hearts out to the songs displayed on a screen, accompanied by Douglas Reeve on the enormous organ that rose up out of the stage. I have kept this love of the theatre all my life, developing a love for the ballet in particular, and all live theatre including being members and attending the Chichester Festival throughout the summer season for many years.

My Aunt's backyard at Number 3 was small, about the same as ours at Number 9. However, it was different in that it was full of tall white daisies and other sweet, smelling flowers. Ours was full of chicken and nothing much else. I suspect that the flowers seemed exceptionally tall to me now because I was still a small child and I remember being able to hide in them and not be seen. Being small didn't prevent us from scrumping the Victoria plums from the tree overhanging from the garden that backed on to Number 3. On one occasion we were caught by the owners and a loud voice shouted out "keep your thieving hands off my plums". We

Eddy and Margaret on Brighton Pier, our 'London Aunt and Uncle'.

shot off indoors and watched from the window; nobody appeared, and we heard no more about it. We were much more cautious the next time we helped ourselves, although it was a little more difficult in the dark.

Mum told me a story about Aunt Clara which still makes me smile. She was an air raid warden and fire watcher in the war which meant she had to be out all night to help with any emergencies and to ensure, amongst other things, that the population in our area were conforming with the total blackout regulations of no light coming from any property.

One night, bombs had been dropped in the railway tunnel sidings beside Elm Grove school. All the surrounding windows had been blown-in and some damage done to various surrounding properties. At the end of the night, Aunt Clara came home completely exhausted and went straight to bed without removing any of her clothes. The house was in complete darkness as the blackout curtains were still shut. When she awoke after many hours sleep she got up only to find she had been fast asleep on the rubble from the ceiling that had collapsed during the bombing raid. She had been so tired she hadn't even noticed.

To earn extra money my Aunt took in holiday makers for bed, breakfast and evening meal. I was treated as if I belonged to my Aunt and was given plenty of treats by visitors. One couple that came to stay was a Mr and Mrs Legg and they joined our family in a roundabout way. They knocked on my Aunt's door looking for somewhere to stay and were invited in and stayed for a week. It was a year later that they made contact with my Aunt again in the hope of making another visit. Unfortunately, she was already booked up solid. On hearing this my Mum decided to go into the B&B business. God knows what she was thinking of as we were already packed in like sardines in our tiny house. Remember we had no bathroom or inside toilet. Our couple seemed to be quite posh and sophisticated compared to us but stayed for a week and, for many years to come, returned time and time again to stay with us including every Christmas and became our 'London' Aunt Margaret and Uncle Eddy. This arrangement was wonderful for us children as we all were given a 10-shilling note at the end of every stay and on our birthdays, a small fortune to us. I still shake my birthday cards, you never know!

Aunt Clara in her Salvation Army uniform.

Aunt Margaret used to send us a bundle of comic papers every week including The Dandy, Beano, Film Fun, Radio Fun, Champion, and many others. It must have cost her an absolute fortune not to mention the postage costs. When my sister was born on May 6th 1947, Aunt Margaret became her godmother and was given the name of Margaret.

As we all grew and headed for young adulthood, Mum, with Dad's blessing, decided that we needed a bigger house as it was becoming more and more difficult with Grandad now living with us following Nan's death. My sister Margaret was getting to the stage where she needed her own space. Number 96, Havelock Road, on the other side of town was the destination which was found for us. It was a far from modern property, but the rent was affordable and had three large bedrooms and a room on the ground floor for Grandad. The house also had a bathroom which was carved out of one of the bedrooms. Just inside the entrance door sat the most enormous copper hot water boiler, and lighting this was a dangerous and cleaver work of art for which you had to be light on your feet. The pilot light was on a hinge and had to be lit before pushing it into the main body of the boiler to enable the main gas ring to be lit. It was at this point that you had to move swiftly to one side to prevent being set alight by the explosion which took place to complete the firing process. We had hot running water for the first time, even if we did have to take our lives into our own hands to get it.

I was to be separated from my Aunt Clara for the first time in my life and it was a difficult time for me as I missed her terribly. At first, I visited her every day as I was biking to school and diverting via her house was not such a big problem. To my shame and continuous regret to this day I began to visit her less and less. The thoughtlessness of youth is my only defence, which I know is no defence at all. I have wished so many times that I could turn the clock back or to talk to her just one more time to say how sorry I am. If she had lived longer I could have made sure I had at least tried to have repaid the enormous debt I owed to her, but of course there is no turning back. She never once complained or said any unkind words to me, I loved her then and I still love her now. What an amazing person.

On my 21st birthday I arranged to pick up my Aunt to come to our new house at 43 Jevington Drive, Brighton, to celebrate with the rest of our family and friends. She was so excited sitting in my first car with me. I took a long drive so that she could see all the countryside around the Brighton racecourse and out to Woodingdean, I could see that time was starting to take its toll on my Aunt and she was looking quite frail. After many years of happiness together my beloved Aunt Clara died on April 7th 1967 after being found at the bottom of her staircase and taken to the Royal Sussex County hospital. By this time I had met Jennifer, my wife, and she came with me to see her. She was not conscious, so I just sat with her for a while remembering all we had done together. As I sit here I can smell her Snowfire face cream she always smelt of, and see the clear glass beads she hung around her neck along with her hair in a bun, and that look on her face. She was a devoted member of the Salvation Army, the same as my Grandmother, and I have photographs of her in her uniform. I often get them out just to look at and remember. I think of her every day at some point and thank my lucky stars that sent her to me and Mum all those years ago.

How lucky to have the love Aunt Clara gave me without ever asking anything in return. I know that when it is my time to depart from this world and if there is anything after, she will be at the front of the queue waiting for me.

Chapter 3
Parents

My Dad, William John Constable (Jack) was born on November 11th 1906 at 11 Herbert Street, Brighton. Although Dad was the first born in his family, life was always very tough for him. He was a very mild-mannered and respectful man, 6ft 1 inch tall and as strong as an ox. Dad's early life was a struggle not helped by his father who spent most of the family income in the local pub. Once drunk he would become violent and use his leather belt on Dad and, later, on all the children.

There are several stories that involve my Dad, the first being one that affected him for the rest of his life. He left school at the age of 12 and managed to obtain many different jobs until he became a butcher's boy at Five Ways, off Ditchling Road, Brighton. After a period of time from when he commenced the job money started to disappear from the till. Straight away, accusations were made against dad, the police were called and soon after he was charged with stealing the money. Dad denied any involvement and no evidence was available to prove Dad had taken the money. This made no difference at all and he was duly taken to court and found guilty on circumstantial evidence, i.e. the money started to disappear only after he joined the butchers. He was given two choices, one to be sent to Borstal, a young person's prison, or he could join the army. One problem may have been a sticking point, my Dad was too young to join the army. However, this was resolved easily by the authorities, they simply put his age on and joined him up anyway. As it turned out Dad chose the wrong alternative, as shortly afterwards it was discovered that the manager of the shop had been syphoning off

My father 'Jack', William John Constbable.

23

My father aged about 16 (circa 1922), The Royal Sussex Regiment.

the cash. Unfortunately for my Dad it was too late as he had taken the King's shilling and there was no way back. Consequently, he became a member of what he insisted on calling THE ROYAL SUSSEX REGIMENT with an emphasis on the 'THE'. Following the completion of his basic training he was on his way to Ireland to fight against the Republican movement, not a good place to be at such a young age. His army records which I obtained years later show his birth date as November 11th 1904, not 1906. I did manage to talk to Dad about his time in Ireland and he said that while there he was based in Enniskillen, County Fermanagh. The women particularly were very unpleasant as they would come up to him and spit in his face and make some awful remarks, which may not have affected the older soldiers but again being so young he took it all very personally. One of the other things he said was that the IRA (Irish Republican Army) soldiers would hide in the roof spaces of the houses and remove a brick from the outside wall, fire shots at the British, including him, and return the brick to its position before their whereabouts could be spotted. After a 10-month tour in Ireland he was told he was to be transferred to India.

I am not convinced he did much fighting against the tribesmen in the Kyber Pass where he was stationed, but his stories to us children said he did. What I do know from his army record is that he was a batman to a senior officer and had an immaculate record of service: honesty, trustworthiness and exemplary conduct.

Another one of Dad's stories was when he was on guard duty and heard a noise approaching. "Halt who goes there?", he called out. No answer. Again he shouted, "Halt who goes there?". With no response to the second call, he raised his rifle and fired in the direction of the noise. When a scream went up, he ventured forward to see who he had shot only to find a dead monkey with a bullet hole in it, which had fallen out of a nearby tree! Other stories included being promoted to sergeant and busted, but no reference to this is in his records. On reflection, years later, I simply don't know which were true and which were a figure of my Dad's imagination. As I have written before, the Constables could always tell a good tale.

Dad had numerous tattoos on his body including a very dark peacock on his right arm which, as I recall, he said had a name and picture of an Indian lady which was hastily covered by the peacock when he met my mum. His records show that he was for some time a member of the military police known as the Redcaps during his 6 years in India and had applied to join the Indian regular police at the end of his term. His idea was to return home to England for a period of leave to see his family, and his devoted mum, in particular and then return to the police force in India. At this point fate stepped in soon after he arrived home. It was at his brother Charlie's wedding when he met this rather attractive young woman who went by the name of Mildred Taylor. I have photographs of this lady who was the epitome of fashion and good looks. I certainly understand why he was besotted by her, but then I suppose I am a little biased towards my Mum.

After a very short period of time my Mum married my Dad at St Saviour's Church, Ditching Road, Brighton on April 3rd 1937. Many, many, years later I was in my 40s, and after celebrating their wedding anniversary a year earlier than it was, we were told that Mum was pregnant with my brother Jack when they were married. Of course, it didn't make any difference to us but it did to my Mum and I could still feel the shame she felt when she eventually told us. She had always drummed into us the importance of not being put in the same position as her and Dad. I used to ask both my parents the question when I was a teenager, "would you both marry each other if you had your time over again", and the answer was always no. Why I asked this so many times is something I have dwelled on over the years, did I have some idea of the circumstances under which they were married? Were they unhappy with each other? Did they feel forced to do something they both did not want to do but parental pressure made them? All these questions have intrigued me for such a long time, and I have to console myself with the fact they stuck together and cared for each other right to the end, for which I and I'm sure my brothers and sister are eternally grateful.

Us children were born at regular intervals during the 1930s and 40s, a period of poverty caused by the great recession and the Second World War. Very little work was available, especially in the construction industry where Dad was now working as a bricklayer. This was heavy physical work. That and the lack of nourishing food affected him with suffering from boils and carbuncles, some of them on his backside. He managed to get a job in Lewes some 20 miles away from home and the only way of getting to work was by bicycle. Off he went on his first morning. By the time he had got to Lewes the boils and one carbuncle had burst, unbelievably painful. He worked all day and rode all the way home again. Dad could, and would, never have let his own discomfort and pain prevent him from earning the money which we so

My parents on their Wedding Day, April 3rd 1937, Brighton.

desperately needed to feed us all. He continued to cycle the journey for weeks to come, with mum washing and dressing his wounds every morning and night in order to ease his pain.

Another time Dad was working on a project in Brighton laying bricks in a line of bricklayers. They were laying bricks in what was called the 'nose bleeding course', the bottom course where the bricklayers were laying bricks. They had to bend right over continually to reach the bottom and sometimes caused the men's noses to bleed. One man stood up to stretch his back and to ease the pressure on his head, at that moment the foreman on the site came around the corner dressed in his bowler hat and waistcoat, as they did in those days. "What are you standing up for?", he shouted. The bricky replied he was stretching his back etc. "Not in our time. We don't pay for stretching your back, you can collect your cards" (his employment documents). The man was instantly dismissed. Things were so bad that men queued outside building sites every day in the hope of obtaining work. As Nan Constable used to say years later, "don't talk to me about the good old days, they were bloody hard", and believe me she would know.

One of Dad's sidelines was as a bookie's runner for a man by the name of Alfie Gilliam who lived in the next street over from us. I was in the same class at school as David Gilliam, one of his sons. Dad's job was to collect all the betting slips which had been deposited with the paper sellers around the town by the betting public. On-street betting was illegal and so it was carried out illegally in this way. After collecting all the slips one day Dad was bringing them all back to Alfie's house along the Queen's Park Road. When he got to the top of Alfie's road, Dad could see that a police car was parked outside the house. At this point Dad broke into a trot and then once out of sight started to run. When he reached our house he called out to Mum who came rushing towards him thinking the worst, like something had happened to one of us children. Dad explained what was happening at which point Mum grabbed all the betting slips and went straight to the copper boiler in the scullery, which was alight due it being a Monday washing day, and in Mum's words "stuffed them all inside and burnt them". In a matter of about 30 seconds, no evidence was left and without that no proof was available, always providing Alfie kept his mouth shut, which he did. It was a close call. If Dad had not been wide awake and bolted, and Mum had not had the presence of mind to act quickly, it could have been a very different outcome. Nobody ever told me of what happened to the bets.

Dad got himself a job with British Railways and when the war came not only was he too old to join-up but he was in what was classed as a reserved occupation and was turned down when he went to volunteer for his old Royal Sussex Regiment. His job was to help to clear up and repair damage to stations and goods yards bombed by the German Luftwaffe. This was a dangerous job when he was occasionally caught out when the bombing was going on.

After the war came to an end, Dad had seen enough death and destruction to last him a lifetime and decided to leave the railways. I must have been about 5- or 6-years-old at the time. I say this as I remember him meeting me from school one day at mid-day and he would not have been able to when working in private business. I could see him coming down the road and made a run towards him. I can see him now with his arms out-stretched, over I went taking a large piece out of my right knee. He picked me up and carried me home for Mum to fix me up; I cried all the way. I can still see the scar as I sit here and feel my Dad's arms around me; wonderful, just wonderful.

After a job with a house builder, Dad joined a company that went by the name of James Longley and Company Ltd, who were based in Crawley some 30 miles north of Brighton, who had a reputation second to none in the construction business. They were to become a very large part of my life much later on. James Longley was the largest private contractor in the area and owned by the Longley family headed by a very charismatic figure by the name of Mr Norman Longley, more of him later. As Longley's were a large contractor with a high reputation they attracted business whenever large contracts were available. One big retailer by the name of Plummer Roddis became a regular customer soon after Dad joined the firm. It was on these projects that Dad built his own reputation in places like Exeter, Southampton, Gloucester and Guildford. All these department stores were so large that they took anything up to 2 and a half years to build and were known as 'away jobs'. For obvious reasons they needed to have a crack team on them, and Dad was chosen as being the person to control all the brickwork involved.

So off Dad went, working away from home and leaving Mum to raise us on her own. At first Dad came home every week but this soon became every 2 weeks and sometimes longer. I hated Sunday evenings when it was time for him to leave. My Uncle Charlie, Dad's brother, was also in the team and picked up Dad in his car. How Mum managed I have no idea, except to say she was a very strong and determined lady and the family needed money and both Mum and Dad made sure we did not go hungry. What I wasn't aware of at the time was that not only did Dad like a drink but he was a gambler and actually spent a lot of the money he made on that. I loved my Dad and find it very hard to say that he was not always fair and honest with my mum. She never knew how much he got paid. To be fair, men in general were a little like that then. He kept her short of money while he was away and led a life of gambling and drinking. This didn't make my Mum's life or us children's lives as good as it should have been. I don't believe Dad was involved with any other women but there is a story which I found out about a lot later involving my Uncle Sid and Uncle Charlie, but did not involve my Dad.

My Dad and his brothers would live in what were known as 'digs', places where people took in lodgers for bed, breakfast and evening meal and this is the accommodation they used to live in when working away from home. At this particular establishment run by a widow it was a fight at each meal time to sit next to the landlady. On one such occasion Sid put his hand on the landlady's knee under the table, while at the same time Uncle Charlie did the same thing from the other side. They both held hands thinking they were being guided to wherever they thought they wanted to be when they realised what was happening. All hell broke loose as each had been given a strong indication by the landlady that she was interested. I was told this story not by any member of the family but by the carpenter foreman who I worked with many years later, Bert Hygate.

In 1967, soon after I had got married, Dad fell down a deep manhole at Sussex University where we were both working, it was a miracle that he was not killed immediately. I was summoned to the scene to find my Dad deep down in the manhole with the emergency services trying to get him out, a very difficult task as he was in so much pain from his leg which was broken in several places including his femoral shaft. He did recover from his injuries and survived for a few years after, but he was never quite the same. He missed all the fun of his grandchildren, but he did survive to see our daughter who is just able to remember him.

On October 3rd 1973, Dad died in the Bevendean Hospital, off of Bear Road, Brighton. He was very ill from the effects of heavy smoking. They drained his lungs and tried to save him but to no avail. My brothers and I decided to stay with him through the night, Jack and Brian staying with him for the first half and Terence and I to stay the second. I went home and went to bed and when it was time to take my turn sitting with dad I made some coffee in a flask in order that I may be able to give him a drink. When I arrived at the hospital to do my stint my brothers came walking towards me. I thought, why had they left dad on his own before my arrival? When they got close they announced that Dad had just died. To my regret and everlasting shame I had no idea he was so ill. To me he was still the same person who used to playfight with us boys and whose arm we all used to swing off. I cried all the way home to Mum's house to tell her and laid on her bed all night with my arm around her. He was 67-years-old.

I still think of him every day at some time, and I still love him. He affected my life to such an extent, as you will discover later in my story.

My Mum was born on July 17th 1913. Her father was Arthur John Taylor and her mother was Martha Taylor (née Washington). Mum was born somewhere in the middle of all her many siblings, which was probably the reason why she had such a strong character.

At the age of 13, Mum left school and was sent to work in Wilson's Laundry which was north of where Brighton Marina now stands. On her first day she was set to work scrubbing the staircases and the floors. This carried on day-after-day, week-after-week, it must have been incredibly hard work for someone so young. As time went by she gradually moved on to different other menial tasks. Eventually being trained to become, in her words, a 'professional ironer'. Needless to say, I am an expert ironer myself – taught by the expert herself.

Everything that happened in our house revolved around my Mum, she always led from the front and could be quite scary. I was coming home from school one day when I saw a girl with what was known as a 'whipping top', it was a toy which spun on the ground and

My Mum, Mildred, aged about 18 (circa 1931).

was kept spinning by whipping it with a long lace. I decided that I was going to be a pain in the rear and kick the wooden top and make a run for it without realising that the girl's mother was so close by. When I kicked the top her mother stepped in front of me and gave me the biggest whack around the ear, which sent bells ringing in my head (no child protection in those days). When I got home, Mum could see I had been crying and the side of my face was bright red. "What's happened to the side of your head?", there was no hiding anything from my Mum and she wanted to know chapter and verse. No sooner had I told her what had happened, and without removing her apron, she grabbed me by the hand and we were out of the front door and on our way to a showdown with the spinning top girl's mother. We arrived at the woman's house with me at Mum's side. She banged on the door. After a short time, the poor woman appeared at the door. Mum's words are still as clear to me today as they were about 68 years ago. "Did you do this to him?", pointing her finger at me. I could see by the woman's face that she realised she was in trouble. Before the lady was given a chance to reply Mum was at her, "nobody but nobody touches my boys. If you have a complaint about my children, you come and see me". Then in a very intimidating loud voice, "do you understand?". During this outburst I could see Mum getting closer to the woman and I was convinced it was about to come to fisticuffs. The poor woman was deathly white, Mum was never one to get on the wrong side of. By this time a small crowd of people had gathered and were watching the action. I was grabbed by the arm and marched off home.

Mum wore a sack apron on Mondays which was wash day, this was exactly what it was – an apron made out of sacking material. I can see her now standing over the big green mangle, a device with two rollers for squeezing out the water from the washing. Mum being a laundry girl, nobody could match her washing and ironing skills, of which she was very proud. When ironing our clothes she used the kitchen table, with a blanket spread over it, and an old sheet on top. Not only did she do the washing for the whole family, but she took in washing from other people to support the household income. There were piles and piles of it. In the kitchen, over the dining table, Dad had fixed a washing line on which she loaded the washing when it had been ironed. One of the reasons for this was that it was the only room in the house where a fire was kept and was able to air the clothes. Most of the time the line was fine and would carry out its function without incident but then, without warning, when fully loaded, would snap and collapse onto the table. This would occur many times when we were all crowded around the table eating a meal, and we would all be covered in washing. Dad would fix it back up again and it would all happen again a few weeks later. In the end he decided much more drastic action was required and a more substantial cure was needed. One of the ends was fixed to the widow frame with the other fixed with a nail into the wall on the other side of the room. He found the largest nail he could find and drove it into the window frame until it came out the other side and then bent it over to stop it coming out. For the wall end he obtained a very, very large metal pin about 9 inches (22.5cm) long which he drove into the wall with his heavy club hammer. This was fine except that the wall was only 4 inches (10cm) thick. He hit it once too often and the point of the pin shot out the other side in the front room, the room into which nobody was allowed to go. When he went next door he found the pin had burst through the plaster and scattered it all over the precious piano. Dad considered he had found the perfect answer to the problem and the next thing we knew we were all being called into the front room to see his answer. Hanging on the end of the pin was the most grotesque plaster mould of a face which he had painted in some railway green paint he had obtained from his work at British Rail. All of us children just fell about laughing and Mum was beside herself with tears rolling down her face. Dad couldn't for the life of him see what was so funny and it stayed on the hook until many years later. When we moved, we never took it with us. Goodness knows what the new tenants thought of it.

On the bottom corner of our street we had a greengrocer's run by the Barton family who, at the head, was one Harry Barton who quite often got himself into conflict with Mum. We would be sent shopping on occasions to Harry's shop and he would take advantage of this to unload vegetables which had been in Mum's eyes hanging around too long and were of a poor standard. It seems a bit strange when I think about it as Harry was, I think, a bit scared of Mum because when she went into the shop she would inspect everything and ensure Harry only gave her the best of what was available. On one occasion when one of us, I think it was my brother Terence, reported back to Mum that Harry had made a rather disparaging remark concerning her, off she went. When she got to Harry's the shop was full of customers and in she went and told poor Harry in a very loud voice that she didn't pay for poor quality goods and she had no intention in accepting what he had just dished up to her son. She also reminded him if he had anything to say about her or her children it would be in his best interest to say it to her face. If there is one thing that I have always hated it is returning goods back to any shop, and I am convinced I know the reason why.

Harry had a son called Ray Barton who drove a lorry up to Covent Garden every Thursday morning to purchase all the fruit and vegetables for the shop to sell during the following week. At about 4.30pm he would return stacked high and loaded down with boxes and sacks. Unloading was a heavy task, so Ray would recruit some of the older, bigger boys, to help unload the lorry. As my brother Terence was always on the lookout to extend his money-making exercises he made sure he was at the front of the line. I learnt a lot from him and used it later in life. I'm sure that brothers Jack and Brian were involved but I was younger and smaller and wasn't allowed to join in. I do remember however that they were paid some in cash and some in specked fruit, and that I managed to get some of it – the fruit that is. My brothers lost their place in the unloading set-up when my Mum decided to tell Ray that if she wanted her children to eat inferior food she would give it to them herself. Even then she didn't know when to keep quiet. Ray banned the boys for a while but let them back after a short time. Knowing Terence, he probably bribed him in some way. I wouldn't put it passed him.

If my Mum was difficult sometimes it was hardly surprising as Dad was working away from home for long spells and she had to cope with everything on her own. Underneath her strict exterior was an amazing sense of humour, sometimes she would laugh until she cried and her whole body would shake until it hurt. One time just before the football cup final was about to start, and we were all sitting around listening, in she came dressed in long pink knickers with a jumper tucked into them and blowing a whistle pretending to be the referee. She was laughing so much tears were rolling down her face as she jogged around the room.

Many of the stories and memories have been told over the years and have probably been modified, but in general they have stayed the same and one of the reasons for writing this account is to ensure the reality is kept. As I was born in 1943, halfway through the Second World War, I have very few first-hand memories but I have known them for so long that they are, as far as I can remember, all genuine. Brighton is on a direct route to London from the continent of Europe which was occupied by the German armies in the Second World War, so bombing raids were made directly over our heads. When the German aircraft failed to release all of their bombs on London they would wait until they were over Brighton and then let them go. The German Luftwaffe left a trail of terror across Brighton and Hove killing 227 civilians and leaving 510 seriously injured, including many women and children. Twenty thousand homes were damaged to varying degrees. One of the places they often tried to hit was the railway tunnel entrance along the side of our school, only a short distance from our house. Bonchurch Road was hit badly on one of these raids. All the windows in the area would be blown out, so to stop the glass from being blown all over the place it was normal to put sticky paper across the window panes to prevent injuries. Another time was when a stray German fighter aircraft started to strafe our street and Mum was out in the open pushing one of my brothers, probably Terence, up our street in his pushchair. She grabbed my brother and dived in the nearest house while the bullets shot past her.

During bombing raids the warning sirens would sound, a long wailing sound, and when this happened it was time to get into the special metal shelter in our kitchen which was provided by the local authority.

On one occasion it was used for something quite different. Mum had noticed that the tinned milk that she had managed to get was disappearing rather quickly. With a bit of detective work she was able to trace where it was being consumed by following a trail of the milk from the store cupboard to the shelter and in turn the perpetrator of the crime. She caught one of my brothers red-handed.

Obtaining sufficient food for all of the family was a serious problem due to the strict rationing that was in place. We certainly did not have the obese problems that dog the western world today, everyone was as thin as a rake and walked everywhere.

After the war had ended and my sister and I grew old enough to be left to fend for ourselves, Mum decided she would have to return to work to put additional money into the housekeeping purse, so it was back to the laundry and the only thing she knew. Just down the road from us in Bonchurch Road was the 'Sunnybank Laundry' which was where she found her next employment. My sister Margaret and I used to go there after school to watch her through the window by standing on a large stone parked outside the side window. Her job was to feed sheets, or remove them, from an enormous revolving drum called a colander, emitting clouds of steam that ironed them smooth. It took four women to operate this machine, two feeding and two removing and folding them up. We could feel the heat through the window from all the steam filling the room. God knows what it felt like inside the room, all the women's faces glowed red with sweat pouring off them.

We had to look after ourselves from a very early age now that Mum was back working, most children did in those times. Getting into our house was never a problem as the key was hung on a piece of string on the back of the front door and all we had to do was to pull it through the letter box and gain entry. I never did understand where the security was in that. Mum was very protective towards us children, sometimes to her own detriment and it got her in a lot of trouble, but she always did what she thought was right. One instance was when brother Brian wanted to get married before he had reached the age of consent – which was 21 years at the time. Mum was absolutely against my brother's wishes and told him, and his intended bride, so. It caused so much heartache in the family that, in the end and against her better judgement, she gave in and agreed. Dad sat on the fence, but that was nothing new. A few years passed and after the death of their only son from cancer, Brian and his wife Jean were divorced. Who is to say my mum was wrong? I happen to think she was right after he went on to have two further wives and several other relationships.

Another problem which was encountered by Mum's protective feelings towards us was with brother Jack's wife, Jill. I've always got on well with Jill and like her very much and as a teenager thought she was the most beautiful person on earth, and I was extremely jealous of my brother Jack when he married Jill. She was then only an 18-year-old, and maybe that was Mum's problem. I don't think Jill ever understood Mum.

Mum loved us all in her own way, but never once did she ever tell me that she did. Anything that came close to affection was short-lived, even if she gave any of us a cuddle. I don't think showing that you were loved was ever considered. She looked on me as her baby boy and I always thought I was very special to her, this could have been because they say I am so much like her family both in looks and her temperament. If you made an enemy of my Mum deep inside it was never forgiven or forgotten, even if on the surface she would try not to show it. I am exactly the same. I wish I wasn't and I have tried hard not to hold grudges, but I am what I am. I have a saying of 'every dog has his day'. Should I be ashamed of that? Probably, but I'm not. It is who I am.

My brother-in-law, David White, turned up on the scene in about 1965. I didn't take to him at first, but I have no idea why. Maybe it was because my little sister had always been close to me and I didn't like this new intruder! David turned out to be one of the nicest, most generous, members of our family and we get on famously. There is an exception to this when my brothers and I pulled a terrible trick on David during a party at Mum and Dad's. He had had quite a few drinks when it was decided he should be put to bed. We had this horrible little Pekinese dog called 'Middy', short for midnight or something or other, I hated the thing. It smelt revolting, like rotten eggs, and yapped a lot. When we had got David into bed we put the dog in with him where they both settled down for the night. I'm not sure he has ever forgiven us for what we did. Another time David had come to tea and my brother Terence and I found some cream cakes in the cupboard which had started to go off, but decided to put them on the table anyway. When David helped himself and took his first mouthful he nearly choked and still swears blind to this day that we knew and had set him up. If David you ever read this account, you were right, we did know!

The first time I saw my brother Terence's wife, Marie, I was sitting on the top deck of a number 42 bus waiting to go home after a night out at the Regent Dance Hall. I looked down and there she was arm-in-arm with my brother. The crafty devil, I thought, you hadn't told me about her. I took to Marie as soon as I met her and whilst we didn't spend a lot of time in each other's company, only at family get-togethers, we had a special connection and we always laughed a lot, mostly at my brother's expense.

My wife Jennifer's relationship with Mum and Dad was good compared with the other daughters-in-law; she could do no wrong. Dad always took Jen's side against me and anybody else if they got in the way and loved her like a second daughter. I believe the situation was a mutual one. She would take Dad out on trips to Brighton races and other places and if he wanted to come to our house she would be off to get him in her little old car and bring him back.

As far as I know our house was the only one that he visited on his own and would stay chatting to Jen all day and watching all the birds in the garden until it was time for her to take him home. It never seemed to concern him that I was at work all day and that he wouldn't see me. Dad hadn't come to see me anyway, the attraction was Jen and our little daughter Emma.

Mum and I together at 'Leacroft' in the 1980s.

Mum never missed a chance to tell everyone how wonderful Jen was, including the rest of the family. Our popularity with them was not enhanced by this I am sure.

When Dad died it was me that Mum turned to and to be honest I encouraged her. Dad had taken me to one side after his accident and asked me to promise him I would take care of Mum should anything happen to him. I don't know if he did the same with my brothers and sister, but I don't think so as he told me he thought that it was what Mum would want. I had made a promise to my Dad to take care of Mum and she was pleased to have me to help. I took control of her finances and made sure that I sorted out her medical problems. My sister Margaret was also a great help and was always on hand if she was needed.

As Mum got older and less able to look after herself I started to talk to her about the possibility of going into a care home, Oh dear, she was having none of it! I was finding it more and more difficult to cope with being on call 7 days a week, 24 hours a day, as I had progressed in my career to become a director of the company I worked for and had many other commitments, but I made sure it didn't affect Mum. I lost count of the number of times she fell over when out in Brighton and finished up in the Royal Sussex Hospital A&E. She had my office number and my secretary was made aware of her situation and, on one occasion, she even interrupted me at a board meeting when I had to explain the emergency and rush to Brighton. I was very lucky to have such an understanding chairman and colleagues who understood the difficulty I was in.

In the end I just had to say to Mum that the time had come to make better arrangements for her care. I contacted my sister Margaret who immediately agreed with what I had in mind and was instrumental in convincing her to move. I produced a list of possible care homes that were in the Brighton area and decided to take a couple of days off work to visit them all. My number one choice was the Salvation Army home in Hassocks, not far from us, as Mum and her family were all Salvationists. After contacting the home and making an appointment I went there and could see that they were in the middle of a major refurbishment. I was to see the officer responsible for the home and when meeting her I was completely shocked by her negative response. I explained our position and the history of my family's involvement with the movement, Nan Taylor's good works feeding and housing the poor at Brighton Congress Hall. It all amounted to nothing and she took no notice and to be honest was just not interested. During the time I was explaining my case to her she kept diving out of the room to speak to other people, in the end I just told the woman not to bother and that I would find a place that really cared. She went off in a huff without another word. Needless to say, I didn't mention any of this to Mum and just lied by telling her that there were not any vacancies. I could see she was disappointed, but we left it at that.

After spending 2 days visiting all the places on my list I came to the conclusion that I could not let Mum be put in any of them, they were all just so awful, the smell alone put me off. One of the places I visited was very nice and the staff had been very welcoming, but they were full so in desperation I phoned their head office in Lewes. I was told by a very nice lady that they were pretty much full everywhere but did have one room in St Leonards along the coast near to Hastings where my sister and brother Brian lived. I contacted my sister and explained everything to her, without any hesitation she agreed to go and look at the home, so I made the arrangements for us to go along. As it turned out we went separately but we both came to the conclusion that it was the place for Mum to go. It all turned out for the good, Mum loved it and I visited often. Even my brother Brian took an interest and went to see her. I visited her every week, sometimes twice, and she was very happy. She hadn't been there long when she announced that she wished she had moved into care years earlier. I kept my lips tightly together and was happy in the knowledge that she was being looked after properly.

One of the problems that did occur was that Mum had misplaced her false teeth. This she hated more than anything, she was always particular about how she looked, but they were found and all was well.

I continued my trips to Hastings for about 2 years until, early one morning, I got a call from the home to say Mum had fallen over in her room during the night and that she was in hospital. On reaching the hospital an hour or so later she had no idea who I was. I was told Mum had had a stroke in the night and that they were very sorry, but Mum's teeth had been misplaced in the rush to get her treated. At about 6 o'clock the next morning I received another call saying I should get to the hospital as soon as possible as Mum was fading fast. I didn't have enough time and she died before I arrived on February 15th 2001. Margaret was already there waiting for me and we went into Mum's room to see her for the last time and to say goodbye.

It was a very sad moment for both of us. I went close to Mum to look at her face, so young and peaceful in death, and between her lips were her false teeth in all their glory. I didn't know whether to laugh or cry, I knew she would be pleased and I thanked God for that. At this same moment I was taken back to when I was young, when she used to play a trick on me and lay perfectly still and when I moved close to her she would suddenly jump and make me scream. I thought if she does that now it will have to be a double funeral.

Brother Jack and I were the executors of her will and so I phoned him after the funeral to suggest we get together to sort everything out. Without any hesitation he said "no Richard, you have always looked after Mum's affairs. You deal with it as you see fit, just let me know when everything is done". I took that as an enormous compliment from my big brother. He trusted me, for which I will be forever grateful.

Chapter 4
Family, Fun and Surviving

My oldest brother Jack was the only one of us that was not born at Number 9, Baxter Street. His entry into the world was in a flat in Shaftesbury Road, Brighton. It would seem that Mum and Dad moved flats between Jack's birth on August 13th 1937 and I remember Mum telling me the following story. When Jack was a baby he was looked after by the landlady who lived in the flat below Mum and Dad at 43 Warleigh Road while they were out at work. On Monday morning October 10th 1938 Mum took Jack down to the landlady Mabel Burrel to be looked after for the day while she went off to work at 'Wilsons Laundry' in East Brighton. When Mum returned from work she found a police car parked outside with a number of police officers milling around. Soon there was a knock on Mum's door where she found a plain clothes policeman standing there who wanted to know when Mum had last seen the lady who lived in the basement flat. On explaining the situation and answering a number of questions the officer left saying that he may wish to talk to Mum again. What the police had discovered was far more than anyone expected, especially Mum, and left her in some state of shock. One of the occupants of the basement flat, Mrs Aline Badham, after who the police had questioned Mum, was found dead – stuffed into an Ottoman chest. It was immediately found that the lady had been murdered and a warrant issued for the arrest of the husband, George Badham, who was subsequently arrested for the murder but found guilty of manslaughter and only served a 1-year prison sentence.

During the summer, holidaymakers engulfed our home town. Collecting empty lemonade bottles and claiming the deposit on them was a good way of making extra cash. Mum was happy for us to make money, in fact she actively encouraged us. It all helped with the family budget, one way or

A Corontaion street party for our friends and neighbours on Baxter Street (1953).

another. Very few people had cars and so it was safe to play in the street outside, which is where we wanted to be. One of our favourite pastimes was a game where two teams were formed, one to hide and one to seek. It was not for us kids to hide but for us to hide written instructions. One group would write a destination on a piece of paper, fold it up small and hide it on a shop front somewhere. The lead group would have to tell where the first destination was. Our second group would follow after a few minutes and have to discover where the directions were hidden to the next shop front. This game would go on for hours much to the aggravation and complete annoyance of the various shop owners, while hordes of us kids would be swarming all over their shopfronts. We had many other outdoor pursuits like this one and many more indoor ones, as contrary to many peoples' memories the sun didn't always shine in the summer. One of the indoor games was mini cricket played on our kitchen table complete with a miniature bat and wicket, all hand made by our cousin Keith. He seemed to spend more time at our house than his own, although I can't blame him for that as his mother, my Aunt Daisy, was the aforesaid complete horror. Our Keith was a whiz at keeping score with his own homemade scorebook in which he produced a league and all the results. This could go on for days, 5-day tests were nothing to us.

Another thing that kept us occupied was playing proper cricket and football, depending on the season, just up the road from us at Brighton racecourse. Our opponents in these games were what were referred to as the 'Old Men' who were patients from the Brighton General Hospital opposite. I think they were classed as low-risk mental cases just let out for some of their day to keep them occupied. One of the units at the hospital, known as 'H' block, was for the more high-risk patients so these were either just getting over a problem or were kept there because there was nowhere else for them to go. My brother Terence was a bad loser if we were playing cricket, when he was judged to be out he would smash the bat against the stumps and storm off in high dudgeon complaining and explaining the reason why he was not out.

As I have pointed out before we as a family had very little money and all us boys had to stand on our own two feet and provide for ourselves and contribute towards the house budget. Brother Jack, being the oldest, started by getting a paper round at Deveroux's the paper shop, opposite the junction of Elm Grove and Queen's Park Road. Jack had the sharpest brain in the family and went to the grammar school by passing what was known as the eleven plus exam. As the title suggests, it was taken when we were 11-years-old, none of the rest of us passed. Mr Deveroux had the contract to deliver and sell newspapers to all the wards in the hospital, soon to include cigarettes, sweets and many other items that the patients may need. When Jack left school and went out to full-time work, brother Brian took over and when he left, in stepped Terence. Now my brother Terence may not have been very academic when he was a boy, but he was smart, very smart, someone who never missed a trick to make money. He is the only person I have ever known who I would bet on to be able to sell fridges to Eskimos. Terence really developed and expanded what was known as the 'Hospital round'. Anything any patient

*Spectators on the terraces of the Goldstone Ground, Brighton and Hove Albion FC.
My father is circled in the crowd.*

wanted or needed he would provide, including items unknown to Mr Deveroux. As I said, this boy was smart. Entering the mental wards was in my view dangerous, not for my brothers, not for Terence, but definitely for me. Once when he was on his round and in the secure area some patients pounced on him and locked him in the padded cell. He was let out later when he was discovered by a staff member, but it didn't put him off – he just carried on selling his goods as if nothing had happened. When it came for Terence to leave school I was dreading it. I was never as brave or indeed as bright as my brothers when we were young. I liked the idea of the extra money but definitely not the type to be taking any sort of risk with my well-being, and anyway I had my Aunt Clara.

I did inherit one job from Terence and this was for Mrs King who lived near the top of our street. His arrangement was to call in to Mrs King every lunch time from Monday to Friday to see if she needed any shopping from the local shops, if she did the payment was 3d (1.5p) per day. Terence had dug himself in with Mrs King and I think she took me on under pressure from him. She really liked him and I think he knew what buttons to push. Saturday was the big day so after being up at 6 o'clock and doing my paper round I had to be at Mrs King's as early as possible and by no later than 8.30am. The first job was to chop all the fire wood for the next week, followed by scrubbing down the back yard and then the steps and paving at the front of the house. Once all this was completed to her satisfaction it was time to do the following week's shopping which meant going around all the local shops to buy whatever Mrs King wanted. All these tasks had to be carried out to a strict timetable as I had to be ready to start my milk round with our milkman at 10.30am. On completion of the milk round, and me collecting 2/6d (13p) and a bottle of milk to take home to Mum, it was time to make my way to the 'Goldstone' ground, home of my home-town football team, Brighton and Hove Albion FC. I still watch and support them over 65 years later and I am a season ticket holder sitting next to Mathew my son. Joshua and Harry, my two grandsons, are also avid supporters. Purchasing my ticket was easy as the last delivery was at the shoe menders at the bottom of the Elm Grove where I could buy a combined ticket for 1/-d (6p) which covered the entrance fee and a coach ride to and from the ground.

My final amount of income was obtained from delivering the catfish from Mrs Spain, who lived at Number 2 Baxter Street, to her daughter on Tuesday and Saturday evenings. Her daughter had a shop in Brading Road and it was my job to make sure her moggy had its rations for the week. I never did understand why she couldn't collect it herself but never questioned it as it enhanced my income by 3d on Tuesday and 6d on Saturday. Why the different sum? I don't know, but 9d (4.5p) each week was not to be sniffed at and was a tidy sum, and altogether my jobs netted me approximately 13/6d (69p) a week.

Life at home for the family was hard, all crammed into our tiny house, with us children growing at an alarming rate and starting to reach young adulthood. As the years went by the fortunes of the country started to improve and for the new Queen's Coronation in 1953 televisions started to appear in the electrical shops, and one arrived in our street. I can't remember her name, but an older lady moved into the street. Her name has been lost on me over time, but it was her who had a television installed first. This woman must have thought she had moved into such a friendly neighbourhood as she received so much attention and help from the day the television was installed.

Come the Coronation some of our neighbours had managed to wangle an invitation to watch. Those that had not, turned up anyway including all the children. In the room where

Mum, on Coronation Day, with a tray of cakes for the Baxter Street party (1953).

the set had been set up everyone was packed in like sardines and was bursting at the seams. Our new neighbour must have wondered what she had let herself in for. As we all crowded around the 12-inch (30cm) screen we could only just make out the coach going down the Mall in black and white with the new Queen in her Coronation robes. The coach and horses, and the white snowy specks, were darting all over the picture. We all sat there for what seemed like hours until it was all over, eating biscuits and drinking tea – all provided by 'Mrs Can't Remember'. Mum seemed to be one of the leaders in our small community and she always wanted to be in charge (I wondered where I got that from). She organised our street party to celebrate the coronation and for each household to contribute 6d (3p) a week to a fund which she collected every Thursday evening and ticked them off in her collection book. This day was chosen by her for a very good reason, most people got paid in cash on a Thursday and by Friday nobody had much left after paying their rent and buying food, with the remainder being gobbled up by the husbands for the pub on Saturday night.

All the residents joined in on the day, setting up tables down the middle of the street. Some made sandwiches, cakes were bought from 'Laws' the local bakers shop at the bottom of Arnold Street, bottles of fizzy drinks for the children and plenty of beer etc. for the adults. The Mayor turned up with half a jar of sweets, and we all questioned who had nicked the other half. Union Jacks and homemade bunting hung from every house and any other space that could be filled.

Terence also had a job working for the local butcher where people were always queuing up and waiting for their ration of meat, much of which was of dubious origin. Risols were part of our diet which were like burgers made of all the leftovers of, and other parts of, the animals.

Having been a vegetarian for almost 40 years plus I try not to think of what passed through me as a young person, but that was all that was available and we had no choice. My relationship with my older brother Brian was never good and we never saw eye-to-eye. His character was more like my Grandad Constable and he could tell a good tale! I found it difficult, if not impossible, to like or get on with him.

Unfortunately, he died of a brain tumour in his late 60s. I did go to the hospital to see him when he was ill at the end, when for the first and last time we had a friendly conversation. I was later told how pleased he had been to see me and how he appreciated me going to see him, all too late I'm afraid.

The Mayor, with a half-jar of sweets, arrives at the street party. I am on the far left (1953).

～ ∗ ～

Chapter 5
School Days

I have a number of memories of my infant's school (primary school). The first was arriving and realising I wasn't going to like it. All those other children getting attention from my first teacher Miss Lama before me, no thanks. My first friend was a boy whose name was Ivan Attrell. We stayed together through all our school years and long into adulthood when he and his wife were at our wedding. In my second year I was made class monitor and put in charge of the stationary cupboard when I came up with what I thought was a rather enterprising idea. To increase my income and, as at the time I was only a 6-year-old, it was currently at nil, I discovered that kept in the cupboard were a considerable number of large thick pencils, just the sort my Dad would like for work. I have no memory of how they finished up hidden under the floorboards inside the front door of our house where the water stopcock was situated. My next problem was of course how to turn these valuable objects into hard cash and decided on the wrong course of action by offering one to my dad for 2d, upon which I found myself giving him an explanation of where I had got the pencils from. I explained what I had done and was made to return them to where I had found them, not an easy task but I managed to do it without anyone being any the wiser. Dad never did anything but explain to me that what I had done was wrong; big lesson learnt.

As Dad was working for British Railways he was able to acquire a pot of orange paint which looked remarkably like the paint used to decorate the old pullman cars which ran between Brighton and London. Dad intended to use it in our house (this was before the wallpaper incident)! To keep it from prying eyes he had put it under the meat safe on the landing at the top of our stairs. My teacher, Miss Williamson at the time, had managed to get some wooden orange boxes which she intended to turn into bookcases. She then requested that us children ask our parents if they had any odd leftovers of paint which she could use to paint the new bookcases. Being the ever-helpful boy I immediately thought of the pot of orange paint, but also thought that if I asked Dad he would say no. I managed to get the paint pot to school, though I don't remember how because it was very heavy. I do remember that Miss Williamson was delighted with Dad's contribution and on completion of the finished articles she praised

In my choirboy outfit at St Wilfred's Church, Brighton, with my brother Terence on the left.

me again and said the colour brightened up the whole room. I was instructed to pass my thanks to my parents for such a wonderful gift. I told them nothing of the sort and forgot all about it. Some months later Dad made up his mind to brighten up our home by doing some decorating, but where was his paint? Nobody ever discovered until many years later when I told the story to my Mum and Dad, and by that time they both thought it very funny, thank goodness. The lessons learnt by these two stories at such an early age was to keep my hands off of other people's property, especially my Dad's.

Miss Williamson was my favourite teacher, I just loved her, and she liked me, well I thought she did. I have always loved art and still paint water colours (not very well). I just like the process which was encouraged by my teacher. While in her class I produced a painting of Brighton Station with steam trains billowing out steam and smoke and passengers walking along the platform. It was deemed amazing and good enough to be put up on the wall for all the class to admire, my words not those of Miss Williamson. Not long after, the school was visited by a group of people from Brighton Art College who were looking for young artists' paintings to exhibit at Brighton Museum and to attend art classes at the college, mine was selected. My picture was displayed at the exhibition where my whole family were taken to gaze on my masterpiece along, of course, with my Aunt Clara. She was very proud and so was I.

Moving to the junior school was quite a different experience with far more discipline and regimentation. We were taught so many things by rote and I noticed the teachers were less friendly, not a bit like my favourite Miss Williamson. It was moving into the juniors that I met my first love who went by the name of Veronica Hilton. The big problem was that all the boys in our class considered her to be theirs and I was too shy anyway. I was a very nervous boy, not helped by the fact that I had bright red hair and blushed an even brighter red if anyone spoke to me. I kept a low profile and gradually developed my own preservation skills which have since been enhanced. They still remain with me and have saved my skin on more than one occasion over the years. My allegiances to Mrs Williamson gradually dropped off once I progressed onto my new favourite Mr White, he was such a good teacher and kept all us children spellbound with his reading to us and storytelling. I remember him reading 'Wind in the Willows' to us every day in sections and would always leave off at an exciting bit so that we couldn't wait to hear the next bit. It is still a favourite of mine and I still have my own copy and have read it on more than one occasion. Mr White's voice can still be heard by me coming out of the book from Mr Toad and Ratty.

My final year was spent in the presence of deputy head Mr Evans. He was a much older man and was very, very strict. His sole aim in life was to get as many children as possible through to grammar school via what was known as the eleven plus exam. This torture and its ultimate result affected a great deal of children of my age for the rest of their lives, it certainly did mine. As we were war babies the exam seemed to revolve around being able to solve and decipher codes. What good it did when the war was over I'm not sure except maybe the people that set the test may have been stationed at Bletchley Park, but then again maybe not. If you passed the exam you were deemed to be very clever and gained entry into the school with all the best qualified teachers and the best facilities. You even wore a uniform which, if you couldn't afford, was partly paid for by the tax payers, unlike the rest who had none of the advantages of the lucky minority. Us 'Failures', the majority, finished up at what was known as the secondary modern school, a dumping ground for many nervous, unsupported, and a lot of very bright children who had not been given a fair chance, and all at 11-years-old. Even now in 2018 the political Conservative Party still keep trying to reintroduce grammar schools, I can't think of a more ridiculous retrograde step for children's education. I still cannot come to terms with the stupidity of this divisive and minority system: my brother Jack passed, Brian went to a halfway house called the 'Building School' and Terence, Margaret and I went to the secondary modern. Terence and I went to a school called St Luke's. Oh dear, what a dump and what a disaster for the majority! Set in the middle of Brighton, in a pretty poor area, poor facilities (well, not poor, we just didn't have anything), no green space, a yard at the back, just a Victorian building without sufficient class rooms and in a poor state of repair.

To top all this a system of corporal punishment was in place, which basically meant we boys (it was a boys-only school) could be beaten with a leather strap. This was known as 'The Tools' and was about 1 meter long and 40 cm wide with strands of leather like a cat's tail. The punishment was at the whim of any teacher, and most did. Administering this punishment was by hitting us across the hand. If you moved your hand you were given extra lashes. It was almost worth moving to see the pain on the teacher's face when 'The Tools' went crashing against his leg. All this at the same time as horrendous bullying by older pupils towards the young vulnerable weaker children. Thank God all this has now been mostly eliminated, but I'm sure that those of my generation who had to endure this child abuse have never got over it and are scarred in many ways because of the treatment many received.

In my first year at the comprehensive school I was completely sickened by what I had got into, but I managed to keep under the radar of all that I could see going on around me. My friend Ivan and I linked up with two other boys, Fred Lankstead and Clive Boyle. We all stayed friends for many years and I still exchange Christmas cards with Fred and his wife Rita, I was their best man at their wedding.

When walking home from school in the first year I for some reason got into an argument with another boy in our class from the next street to ours. His name was Terry Williams. We were both about the same size and I thought I could handle him, which on reflection I'm sure I could have done, on his own. We got into my first and last fight until much later in my life, more of that later. All was going well, and I was getting the better of him, until his best friend, Micheal Swindells, came on the scene, he was a pretty big lad. Now I had two of them on top of me and I was trying my best to get free to make a run for it but they had me pinned down with punches coming from all directions. Suddenly I was picked up by both of them and thrown against a nearby wall. I swear I heard the crack as my left knee hit the wall. I think my assailants must have heard it as well as they legged it away as fast as they could. My left knee started to swell in front of my eyes. I managed to get to my feet and hopped home holding onto the garden walls along the way, by this time I was in extreme pain. When I eventually got myself home, to my relief my brother Jack was there. He soon saw I had a problem and got a flannel and soaked my knee in cold water in the hope that it would help reduce the swelling. We waited but the pain was getting worse and the swelling was not going down so Jack decided that we were going to A&E, at the very top of Elm Grove. Our next problem was how to get there as I couldn't put my left leg to the ground. Jack decided there was only one way, so he hoisted me on his back and carried me all the way with my leg hanging out the back.

What a hero my big brother was that day. I was nearly strangling him, but he carried me every inch of the way. To our astonishment the doctor who saw me decided it was only bruised and sent us home with no ambulance, no help – so much for the wonderful new NHS. Jack carried me all the way home and even managed to carry me up the stairs and lay me on the bed. My leg was so painful it still brings tears to my eyes thinking about it.

All night I was in pain and Mum decided that I should return to the hospital. I cannot for the life of me remember how we managed it. This time I saw a different doctor who decided to take some X-rays when it was discovered I had split my kneecap in two. After it was set back in position my whole leg was encased in plaster from my hip to my ankle to stop any movement, and that's how it stayed for the next 10 weeks.

My Mum knew straight away why I had been hurt so badly. She said that against her better judgement she had done something wrong by going to the cinema on the previous Sunday. She also considered it against the Lord's wishes to knit, sew and play cards on Sunday – all of which she observed meticulously.

Mum, when she saw me, said that my accident and my pain was her fault and the good Lord was punishing her for going to the cinema on a Sunday. I have never understood the logic that in some way she was being punished, it was my knee that was hurting, and I hadn't been to the bl**dy cinema!

Michael Swindells' mother was beside herself with Michael's actions so around she came to our house with the perpetrator of the crime, carrying with him all his best comics, books and games which she made him give to me. Once he had handed them all over, and to complete his humiliation, he was told to tell me how sorry he was for what he and his horrible accomplice had done to me. But that was not all. Mrs Swindles then informed her Michael that he was to visit me every other day to check how I was and to see if there were any other of his prize possessions I would care to have. I would like to have said to him that two against one does not pay, does it Michael, but settled for all his best gear. I'm not sure he liked me finding out what other goodies he had by asking him in front of his mother and then him having to hand over his precious things or helping myself to his weekly sweet ration; but that's life, you do wrong and you pay the price.

Eventually the day came for me to return to school after having had the plaster removed from my leg followed by an intense course of physiotherapy. After one of the physio sessions I had to return to school where I met up with my class in the school canteen, which was being used due to a lack of classrooms. Our teacher was a very large strapping young man by the name of Mr Chadburn. He disliked me and my friends and we had already decided that we hated him but we were stuck with each other. It was half way through the lesson when I arrived back and was greeted in Chadburn's normal friendly way, "Constable sit down", and not wishing to finish up in trouble sat down next to my friend Ivan, that was probably my mistake. Ivan whispered to me "was I OK?", to which I simply whispered back "yes". Without any warning Chadburn was on to me, "Constable come out here, you're talking". I didn't move as I could see what was coming, he was getting out 'The Tools'. Again, he shouted at me to go out to the front of the class. With that, my mate Ivan was on his feet, "you leave him alone" he shouted. "He has only just come back from the hospital and didn't say anything anyway". "You can come out as well then", was the reply. Within seconds Ivan was in front of him before I had begun to move. I thought Ivan was going to submit and then it would be my turn, but oh no, my mate was not going easily. Instead, Ivan took an enormous swing with his fist at Chadburn's chin, missed, and hit him straight in the eye, all hell broke loose. Our teacher was trying to restrain Ivan by punching him and Ivan getting a punch and a kick in where he could and the whole class making things worse by singing and chanting and generally causing mayhem. In the end it all fizzled out and Ivan was taken battered and bruised to the headmaster's room.

We never saw Mr Chadburn again. Ivan and I had been questioned along with other class members by the schools' Inspector who decided it was all Chadburn's fault. He was suspended and then fired from his job. After school finished for the day my mate and I went home to his house to celebrate with cold drinks and thick slices of bread covered in jam, all supplied by

Mrs Attrell. I liked her a lot. She was a very strict, tall, rather large lady who was always dressed immaculately and wore a fancy hat when out. Two years after this event, Ivan's mum died of cancer when he was just 13-years-old, what a tragedy. He struggled with the after effects of her death for many years to come. My Mum tried to help and invited him, as I did, to our house as often as he wanted to come. You could see he missed his mum and desperately wanted a mum of his own and started calling my Mum 'mum' instead of Mrs Constable.

As much as I liked watching football I was completely hopeless at playing it. I don't know why, I had good co-ordination skills and could do most things, but football was not one of them. Ivan, Fred and Clive were good at the game and played for the school team but as much as I tried it was not a game for me. Mind you, I still don't like the idea of being kicked around in the name of sport, so it was probably this that was the truth behind my lack of skill in the football department. Not playing the game cost me a lot of opportunities to play other sports as our PE teacher assumed I couldn't.

An opportunity came up at school which allowed certain pupils to go on what they called an outward-bound course. This consisted of a bike ride around Sussex over a few days using an ordinance survey map. By this time I had my own bike, and so did Fred, but Ivan and Clive didn't so I thought I would have a good chance of being included. By the day of selection I had convinced myself that I would be chosen. Those picked were read out in alphabetical order: Attrell, Boyle 'C' was next up and to my horror it went straight to Lankstead. I pointed out to the PE teacher that some of those chosen hadn't even got bikes so why had I been left out? It did no good at all, the reason he gave was that I wasn't any good at sport so I wouldn't be going. Don't feel sorry for me at this point because later I proved him wrong and made him eat his words in more ways than one: every dog has his day.

Revenge came soon after my mates had set off on the trip when a whisper went around the school that Ivan and Clive had gone missing on their borrowed bikes and the police had been called in. Two days passed without any news and it had all got a lot more serious with teams of police out looking for the lost boys. By day three everyone was getting very worked up and emotional when a report came through that they had turned up at Clive's house. When asked what had happened they had replied that they had got tired of cycling so had decided to head home. Hardly surprising if you don't own a bike and are not used to riding, I thought. On the return to school the following week, Ivan and Clive were summoned before the headmaster to be interviewed about what had happened. Following this they were taken in front of the whole school at morning assembly and further humiliated. Did I feel sorry for them? No, not really. After they had it explained to them how they were a disgrace to the school and not to expect to be included in any further events, they were dismissed to lick their wounds. Our PE teacher we heard was also taken to task for selecting boys who were not used to bike riding. If they had asked I could have told them that at the outset.

Not long after our form master, Mr Tanner, 'Bob' to his friends (for those younger readers our old currency included a shilling and a sixpence which had slang names of 'Bob' and 'Tanner' hence the name 'Bob'), asked our class if anyone would like to have a go at playing badminton. I had never heard of the game let alone how to play it, but shot my hand up straight away. I had been waiting for this chance. As soon as the racket was put in my hand I knew I would be able to play the game. Amazingly, I could play a sport at last and soon picked up the rules. After a couple of sessions our PE master was invited along to play. I played doubles against him with 'Bob' and we beat him out of site. I cannot begin to tell you of my total joy in putting him squarely in his box. I just had one other thought which was no matter who I played each stroke was to prove that I should have gone on the outward-bound course. I never forget. I went on to play badminton for many years after enjoying every minute of proving our PE master wrong.

My next opportunity to prove my nemesis wrong was when he decided to introduce us to basketball. I sat listening to him explaining the rules. By this time I was about 13 and heading towards 6 feet tall so, on this alone, I was one of the first to be chosen (I think he had learnt his lesson). Fred was the first chosen. That's it, I thought, that's me done but no I was next up, chosen above everyone else in my school year. It turned out that I was not only good I considered myself the best at the game and went on to play for the school team against all the other schools in Brighton and the surrounding area. We won all the competitions we entered.

Thinking about this episode in my life years later, I did play football with my mates for hours after school in the Queens' Park but was always last to be picked when the teams were chosen. This may have destroyed my confidence in any ability I may have had. I loved the evenings we played football, after playing for hours and on hot summer evenings we would jump on our bikes (Ivan and Clive got one in the end), and head for the seafront. We always swam on 'Daltons' beach, where we would drop our bikes, strip off our clothes, and run straight into the sea. What bliss. I remember on one occasion it was pouring with rain and a massive thunder storm raging with lightning streaking over our heads. We did just the same, dropped our bikes and clothes under the space beneath the promenade and rushed straight into the sea, danger what danger?

Unfortunately for my brothers and I, school was not confined to 5 days a week. Unlike all sensible families, we had Sunday school and the church choir to attend. Mum considered it too far to travel to the Salvation Army like the rest of her family, so we were sent to the local church, St Wilfred's, at the bottom of our road. St Wilfred's was classed as Anglo Catholic, Church of England but following the traditions of the Roman church, and attendance was expected morning and evening. Attendance in the morning for Sunday school, and the church service in the evening for what was known as the Evensong service. Wednesday evening was choir practice night. To be honest I hated it but had my interest maintained by the small sum of 2/6d (12p) we received every 3 months for singing in the choir. We did have one extra perk which was to be taken by Mr Pollard, our choir master, on a walk to the seafront after the Sunday evening service to have a 6d ice cream from Gizzy's Ice Cream parlour at the bottom of St James's Street and then onto the 'Banjo' groyne.

Chapter 6
Work

Christmas 1958 arrived, and the time had come for me to leave school. I was just 15-years-old on October 14th 1958, and we were expected to leave school at the earliest possible time, the nearest term end in which you attained the leaving age.

Secondary Modern schools were not to educate children to a very high standard and we were not given any chance to take exams. Irrespective of what standard you had reached you were simply shunted out of the door with hopefully a reasonable grasp of reading, writing and arithmetic and if you had attained that then you considered yourself very lucky. What an awful waste of potential talent and young lives. Planning for leaving school was non-existent, there wasn't any, you were on your own, although there was a place you could go called the youth employment office. This was completely useless and anyway there were no jobs for young people to be employed in.

I remember my Mum asking me what I was going to do to get a job, to which I replied that I didn't know. Her response was quick and to the point, "You need to find a job and quick, if not, how are you going to pay your keep?". Her meaning was how was I going to fund myself and contribute to the family income. She wasn't being unkind in any way, that was just the way it was and what was expected of you. Getting that elusive first job was a cut throat business, there were just so many young people chasing anything that became available.

I decided to go along to the Youth Employment Office run by Brighton Council where I was interviewed by a very pompous woman who didn't seem particularly interested in her own job, let alone helping find one for me. After a lot of huffing and puffing on her part I was sent to a clothing manufacturer called 'Harrimon's' in the rare hope that they may be willing to see me. I went but it was hopeless. I was put in a room with many others and left to sit there for over an hour, I wasn't surprised that I was not offered a job. My friend Fred, funnily enough, did get a job there and spent most of his working life cutting out clothes for a pittance.

I kept looking and hoping something would turn up, scanning the newspapers and asking around – all to no avail. In the end it was Mum that found me a job. She had met Uncle Bill

Levett, who was married to my Mum's sister Aunt Lou. Uncle Bill was the general manager of the 'British Railways' carriage works at Lancing just along the coast. I was taken on as a trainee coach builder at the grand sum of £2-5s-0d (£1.25p) per week, Monday to Friday. My outgoings from this sum was £1-0-0d for my keep to Mum, leaving £1-5s-0d to clothe myself, to pay for the cost of my tools and anything else Mum would not pay for. Toothpaste came into this category as she considered anything like that as 'personal' and not an expenditure that should fall on other contributors. There was no argument, that was her rule even if she made them up as she went along.

Before I was officially appointed to the job I had to have a medical at Brighton station, a bizarre experience with particular interest in whether or not I was colour blind. I had to pick out numbers from millions of coloured dots on a sheet of paper and having to strip off and cough while the male doctor held my private parts and inspected my rear end. I just submitted to all this as I was desperate for the job, but I did not like it and felt very uneasy. I was only a 15-year-old, remember, but then again it was Brighton!

Work started at 8am so it was up at 6 o'clock and a walk to the station. Later it became a little easier when I was allotted a seat on the special works train which delivered the workers right into the carriage works. If you were late you were deducted money from your wages for each quarter of an hour, and to monitor this I was issued with a round lead disc with an identification number on it. It was handed in to a checking point at the start of the day and handed back when you finished, so that your times could be checked.

My first place of work was in a small workshop above the sawmill, a dirty smelly dusty room full of grime which floated up from below. I was introduced to the only person in the room, his name was Reg. He seemed very old to me, was so strict and made me earn every penny of my wages. Our job was to sharpen all the blades, metal cutters, and circular and band saw blades used in the machinery in the mill. It was the lowest of the low of jobs. My eyes became very sore from all the dust and my hands encrusted with grime and oil. Today, at the age of 15 you are classed as a child and such treatment judged illegal, but then it was quite normal. My brother Terence was in an even worse position but that would be for him to tell, except to say that he told me years later that he was once at the point of despair and sat in a large metal box he was helping to build as an apprentice sheet metal worker and cried his heart out all alone. I have never forgotten the desperate look on his face as he told me his story, him being so upset was only part of it.

One of the first lessons I learnt was how to make a bit of extra money on the side. I had to take orders from all the men in the mill for bread rolls, tea and other food to be collected from the works canteen. I was given a wooden box for collecting food and a metal can for the tea. All went fine for about a week, and I liked the idea of getting away from the mill for a time. Cheese rolls were 3d each and plain rolls only 2d. Now my trick was to order the same number of plain rolls as cheese ones, then on the way back to the mill switch half the cheese to the plain ones and bingo I had made a profit of 1d on each transaction. I also worked out that the tea run could also produce a profit. In order to do this, I purchased tea tickets for each cup of tea and handed them over to the man who used them to dispense the tea from a set position in the works. After about a week I reduced the number of tickets by one even though I still needed the same number of cups of tea. By this time, the tea man had become used to filling my can and did so leaving me with a penny profit. As the weeks went by I gradually reduced the number of tickets while still getting a full can of tea, increasing my take at the same time. Everything went well for weeks until one day my tea man only half filled my can. He had rumbled my scam and I had to cough up more tea tickets. I couldn't complain. I had done well and learnt a good lesson and had much more to learn.

After 3 months I was told that I was to move down into the mill itself, replacing the boy who had gone before me. If the workshop with Reg was a God forsaken hole then the mill was hell on earth. Health and safety was not important, had it been then the whole place would have been shut down. It was in the mill that I was taught how to set up the wood cutting machines and install the cutters etc. that I had been sharpening and preparing with Reg. Some of the men who operated the machines were very strange and as a boy I was frightened to be near them. Some of the boys who had gone before me were treated to all sorts of punishments and so called initiation ceremonies. Nobody tried anything with me, I was over 6ft tall and a very serious boy and made sure they understood to keep away from me.

It soon became apparent to me that I had to look out for myself in many ways, including not being seriously injured by one of the ancient machines. To enable train coaches to be linked together from a distance without getting under the train it required a long-shaped pole with a hook on one end. The machine used for producing this was in the sawmill and incredibly dangerous. Along the outside of an 8ft drive shaft were bolted a series of sharp metal cutters in front of which a long piece of square timber was placed parallel with the cutters. Operating the machine was simple. Once the wood was in position, you just lifted a handle which set the cutters and the wood spinning. As they both met each other, the pole was produced to the shape required. All this was fine except there was no protection for the operator in the way of goggles or guards. On the odd occasion, the bolts holding the cutters in place would shear off and allow them to fly in all directions. When this happened, the operator would scream out 'duck' and everyone around just threw themselves on the floor and waited for the danger to pass – then get up and carry on with their own tasks. It only happened once when I was there and thankfully nobody was injured. I laid on the floor until one of the machinist came over to me and told me to get up. I would have stopped there all day. After a further 3 months I was moved on again, this time to the carriage repair workshop, just as dirty but much safer. I had survived the sawmill.

As an apprentice aged about 16.

It was about now that I came to the conclusion that there must be a better life waiting for me and made a promise to myself that I was going to find it and it was time for me to take responsibility for my future. I decided to leave. Telling Mum my intention was not going to be easy and something I wasn't relishing. I knew what she would say and sure enough she did, "How are you going to pay your keep?". I had no answer. My family on Dad's side had all been in the building trade but Dad was dead against any of us boys following in their footsteps and had prevented my brothers from doing so. It was hard dirty physical work and during Dad and Grandad's time poorly paid. Somehow, I had to convince him. I thought the best way was to talk to Mum and let her talk to Dad in the hope that the need for my financial contribution to the household would outweigh her thoughts to side with Dad. I gave my notice in to the railway anyway and hoped for the best.

Mum had the conversation with Dad and they both concluded that if the building trade was what I wanted then I should be allowed to try and was left to my own devices to find a job. What I didn't know was that Dad had decided to help by approaching his boss, a man by the name of Mr Bill Shepherd, who in turn had discussed me with the chairman of the company, Mr Norman Longley (later to be Sir Norman Longley). Dad arrived home from work a week later and told me I was to attend an interview with the company, James Longley & Co. Ltd, at East Park, Crawley, the following Thursday. I was very nervous from the moment I was told and had trouble sleeping, but I also knew that this was my big and only chance and had to do all in my power to get selected. I wanted to look smart and to make a good impression, to give myself the best opportunity, but I didn't have a suit or anything else appropriate to wear. My brother Jack came to my aid once again by offering me one of his suits and all the other attire I needed, pressing the suit and preparing me for my big day. I don't expect he even remembers the trouble he went to to help me, but I do, and it was his kindness to me that made sure that his son Steven obtained an apprenticeship years later when I was able to repay, in some small way, what he did for me.

The big day arrived and I was up, ready and dressed, to go and get the train from Brighton Station to Crawley. All trains in 1959 were run by steam so it was very easy to ruin a white shirt if you sat close to an open window when black soot from the engines burning coal was emitted from the funnel. I sat near the end of the train, as far away from the engine as possible. This was not such a good idea as when the train arrived at Crawley station the rear stopped two carriages away from the beginning of the platform and I had to scramble along the corridor to just get out in time. Getting off the train I made my way up the road to East Park. What I did not know was that the firm owned most of the houses in the road, many occupied by their workers. At the end of the road was a number of large huts which formed what was the head office, all these were replaced with smart new brick-built offices later.

Nervously I knocked on the door marked with a sign reading 'office' and was opened by a tall grey haired man with a roman shaped nose just like Nan and me. I explained who I was and was greeted with a warm smile and then invited inside. I liked him straight away and started to feel at ease. "So pleased to meet you Richard, your Dad has told me all about you." Followed by, "Were you able to find us easily?". I knew I had found my home, all I had to do was to convince this lovely man that I should have a job! Mr Norman, as I came to know him, introduced himself and I knew I was in the presence of a very special person. I had never attended an interview before, so I was not sure what was expected of me or what I would be asked. "Come and meet the team", said Mr Norman, and then he led me around the office introducing me to everyone with the words: "This is Richard Constable, our new apprentice". You could have knocked me down with a feather. At the end of the introductions Mr Norman explained to me that he was very busy and that he would be in touch very shortly to confirm the day and where I should report to. I was then handed over to his secretary who gave me tea and biscuits and reimbursed me with the cost of my fare for the train.

I had left school without any qualifications and was just about able to read and write to a reasonable standard; all that was about to change. I had secured the ultimate for a boy from my working class background, a 5-year apprenticeship with one of the best contractors in the country and all on Dad's reputation. I knew how lucky I was. What took a while for me to realise was that everything had been arranged about my future between Mr Norman, Mr Sheppard (Dad's boss) and Dad. All I had to do was turn up and look smart. How can you thank people like that? I didn't know then that I was to repay them all a hundred times over and some, but that was all in the future.

After a few days a letter arrived telling me that I was to report to a new building site in Crawley which was the first phase of the development of the old cottage hospital. My pay was to be 1 shilling and 2 pence farthing an hour, the going rate for a first year apprentice carpenter/joiner, with 46 hours per week which included Saturday mornings. Every detail of my employment was to be in accordance with that set down in the working rules agreed between management and the building trade unions. I got myself a copy and joined the union just in case I should need it in the future. I trusted my employer, but I have always been one to be prepared for any eventuality.

I arrived on the site way before the 8am start time and reported to the office as instructed. I knocked on the door and was soon greeted in a very unfriendly manner by the site manager Mr (he always insisted being called Mr) Ron Mitchell. I was to find out that everyone on the site hated Mitchell with a vengeance. He was such a pompous, arrogant man who never missed an opportunity to criticise anyone, especially if he considered you were beneath him –

My first project I worked on – the development of Crawley Hospital.

which of course I was. Early each morning he would stand on the tallest part of the building overlooking the site office to watch the workforce arrive, so that he could check up that anyone who clocked in late would have his wages docked, even for a few minutes. The men won, as they always do, and would just band together and clock people in even if they had not turned up that day. Alternatively, they would leave the site early without him knowing and get a friend to clock them out. Mr Mitchell couldn't keep tabs on all the workforce. My experience later in my career was if I treated the men fairly and levelled with them they would respond in a positive way and do anything for me. Funny how you can learn such lessons at such a young age.

Many years later Mitchell's past caught up with him when he was given a project to manage, a very large house for the chairman of one of the major supermarkets. It was a very unusual design for the time in that it was to be constructed in reinforced concrete. Mitchell for all his hot air was short on practical knowledge and he had been able to rely on other people to do all the work on larger jobs, but this one was much smaller by comparison, so he had to do everything himself. Once the concrete frame had been completed the structural engineer happened to notice that a rather large amount of reinforcement was still on site. As there shouldn't have been any he wanted to know why. Mitchell had no idea what was coming until the engineer insisted that a full internal investigation take place to check that all of the required reinforcement had been installed to his design and drawings. It turned out that it wasn't, and that no records were available that my friend had checked it. He had been found out and was instantly dismissed with the engineer insisting that the frame be demolished, and work start again all at the firm's expense. Every project that I was ever involved with on site had regular checks and records kept of all reinforcement placement, any left-over was quickly removed from site. Every dog has his day, and no sympathy from me.

I was introduced to the carpenter foreman whose name was Eric Dunford, a stocky man of about 30, who I knew for many years after, until his wife died suddenly and he went completely to pieces and never recovered. Eric explained what was expected of me and I made sure I understood. I would have done anything they had asked. I was told that I was to work with a carpenter who went by a name I will never forget. Alf Oxborrow was to be my guide and mentor on site for the next 6 months. Alf was, to say the least, a very big man, about 5ft 6ins (1.6m) tall and about the same wide, weighing in the region of 18 stone, he was big! Due to his size, Alf was confined to working at ground level in one corner of the site under a tarpaulin structure where a large circular saw was set up. To enable the concrete structure to be formed, timber moulds called shuttering had to be made and it was this task that had been given to our Alf with me as his helper. Alf's first words to me were "Have you got any tools?". As Dad had managed to buy me a basic set, my answer was "yes" but I had left them at home until I knew what I was going to do. The reply was short and sharp, "They are no f***ing good there are they? Make sure you bring them tomorrow". Oh dear, I was not used to such language from adults and I was about to endure 6 months of misery.

I found out some weeks later that it was all about Alf's son who had been an apprentice with him and had almost completed his time when he was found to have leukaemia and died soon afterwards. It was about the time I joined the site team that this all happened. I truly believe that Alf took out his grief on me, so the first 6 weeks I spent digging out the sawdust that accumulated under the saw. As it was a wet September everything around our area of the site became waterlogged and soon became a sea of deep mud. Nothing was done to ease the situation so I spent all my time pushing a wheelbarrow full of rubbish through the mud to a pile a hundred yards away (95m). It was exhausting work for anyone, let alone a boy of my age, but nothing was going to stop me from staying the course. Mum would have killed me if the work didn't.

One of the great advantages of an apprenticeship was that I was allowed one day each week to attend Brighton Technical College, provided I attended two evenings in my own time. As my formal education had been very basic it was a bit of a struggle for me at first, but I soon caught up and eventually obtained what was called the 'City and Guilds Certificates in Carpentry and Joinery'.

I think Alf came to the conclusion that he wasn't going to put me off and started to give me more interesting things to do amongst all the grot, and I started to enjoy myself. Time passed by and I got more and more into the work until Alf and his workshop were not needed anymore, so we were moved in to the now constructed shell of the building. Following on from the bricklayers who had formed the window openings, we were to fit the windows. This all went well, until we had our lucky escape. It was just before fixing our first window of the day when Alf pointed out to me that the two gas bottles in the room could be dangerous if they were to be knocked over. If that should happen, he said, jump over the wall beneath the window opening as quickly as you can and crouch down which should shield you from any blast. Of course, it was tempting fate – and that's exactly what happened. I made a leap for the wall but was caught across the front by Alf leaping in front of me. Over the wall he went, all 18 stone of him, in one leap – or do I mean heap? I just stood there watching and waiting for the explosion, but nothing happened. It took Alf at least 2 minutes to surface from behind the wall when he carried on as if nothing had happened.

My second project – 'The Metal Box Company', Portslade, East Sussex. You had to be prepared to do anything.

Towards the completion of the building process I was told I was to move on to a new project at 'The Metal Box Company', at Portslade on the coast. This was followed by many others including a new building for the Custom and Excise at Southwick, the first building to be built at Sussex University, followed by the Library and Arts buildings on the same site.

On joining the team at Sussex, I was assigned to work with a much younger man, who went by the name of Brian Moores, who was only about 3 years older than me. Brian was a wonderful man who taught me everything he could and encouraged me in every way possible which made my life so much more interesting. We worked as a two-man team and Brian treated me as an equal. One task we were given was fixing all the bookcases in the offices of the new Arts Building, there were so many it was going to take weeks to do but we were up for the challenge. All the bookcases were pre-made at our joinery works in Crawley to a very high standard and to tight tolerances. Unfortunately, the same could not be said for the brick partitions between which the bookcases had to be fixed. A high-level meeting was called on site between the joinery works management and the site managers to determine what should be done. In the end it was decided that the items of joinery would have to be adjusted on site as no two rooms had been constructed to the right dimensions and it would just not be practical to take them back to Crawley. The ends of the bookcases had to be removed without any damage and adjusted to length, and in most cases the tops removed as well, bearing in mind that everything was tightly glued together and never expected to be ever taken apart again. It was some task.

Brian and I decided that we had to have our own meeting to decide how we could maximise our financial position in the face of such a herculean and responsible task (our words not managements). We decided that the best way was for us to involve the work study department, as we had on many previous occasions, and ask them to do a timed study on how long it would take to adjust the average bookcase and from this a bonus target would be set which meant that any betterment of the set time would be paid to us in the form of man hours at a given monetary rate. Ensuring that the targets were slanted in our favour a certain amount of craft and skill was needed, not to mention high performance acting. Whilst being able to demonstrate that you were working extremely hard while the timing was being carried out, we also had to be doing as little as possible. Brian and I became masters of the art and in consequence increased our take home pay many times.

On the roof of the new debating chamber at Sussex University, with Brian Moores (on the left) and Reg, a colleague.

It all started soon after Brian and I were put together when we were given the task of installing the slatted ceiling to the main refectory in the original Sussex University building. It consisted of fixing long cedar boards with brass cups and screws across the domed ceiling. Our plan was to fix the timbers using normal screwdrivers which was slow and laborious. Once the targets had been fixed and issued to us and after the process of timing by the bonus surveyor, out came our secret weapon: 'Yankee screwdrivers'. These newly introduced tools from America worked on a spiral rod that when pumped up and down drove in the screws at an alarming rate. The result was half the effort and a big fat pay packet. Life was still hard in the industry with no pay if it rained (if you had to stop work) and we still had to clock in and out by putting a card into a timing device to record the hours we were on site and working. If you were off sick from work there was no sick pay, no pension rights and the hours were still long.

Time passed as I became more skilled and experienced and my partner Brian was about to get married and thinking of joining another firm who paid more money, which he eventually did.

When Brian had gone we entered an extremely bad winter period with heavy snow falls and sub-zero temperatures. All the personnel on the site were stood off, on no pay of course, and I was left on my own to fit and hang dozens of windows to the building I was working on. I can't remember feeling so cold. I lit fires in a metal oil drum and even wore my pyjamas under my working clothes, the cold weather went on for weeks. Fortunately for me I was an apprentice so could not be laid off and had to be paid.

The whole 5 years passed quickly and my apprenticeship came to an end. I then had to wait to see if I was to be kept on in my employment, as your employer could just get rid of you if they were not satisfied with your standards or capability. Fridays were always known for the day when anyone could be sacked (made redundant without compensation). No reason had to be given as employers had the power to hire or fire at will. Jobs were few and far between, so being dismissed from your job was something to be avoided at all costs. I can remember workers getting up to all sorts of tricks, including hiding in cupboards to prevent the foreman from being able to find them, or just not turning up for work on the day, anything to try to hang onto their jobs. Fortunately, I was kept on with an uplift in my pay to full tradesman rate

I carried on as I was for about a year before I started to get itchy feet and was up for a new challenge. The work was dirty and tradesmen were not treated with the respect their skills deserved. One Sunday morning while reading the newspaper I came across an advert for the police force and was taken with what was said to be on offer. I thought this may be a way of taking me in a completely different direction. I wasn't sure and so I left it for a while to give myself time to think. I had put a lot of effort and time into my apprenticeship and now had the skills and knowledge of the whole industry which I felt I could put to good use. I talked my thoughts over with my Dad who told me to do exactly what I thought was best for me, he certainly didn't seem to be disappointed with me.

I decided to respond to the advert and see where it took me, 'nothing ventured nothing gained', and I was not making a commitment one way or the other. I applied and received back an application form, completed it and sent it back straight away. Soon after I was summoned to an interview at the Brighton Town Hall where I was given the once over by a senior police officer who, after he had completed questioning me and filling in further forms, told me that I would be contacted again. A short while later I received a further letter asking me to attend the next stage of the process which was a full medical. During the medical, which made the one I had gone through years before at British Railways seem easy, I was measured for my height which had to be over 6ft (anyone under was rejected). This was straight forward as I was 6ft 2in. Next up I had to sit an entrance exam which I passed and then an interview by a board of senior police officers and told that I would be informed in due course of my success or failure. Finally, I was asked for a character reference which had to be from anyone who had known me for a long time and was either a solicitor, bank manager, teacher or similar profession. I didn't know anyone of this sort and asked Dad for advice. I was in luck as he came up with a person he knew who was a Brighton councillor and, not only that but, a member of the council's 'Watch Committee' – the people who oversaw the workings and activities of the whole Brighton police force. I was offered a place on the force soon after, so it was time to make up my mind. I did have doubts about the whole idea, the pay for police officers was not very good and certainly not as high as I was receiving from my trade. Again, I talked to Dad as he always wanted be a member of the police force from the days when he was in the military police when stationed in India and after when he intended to join the regular Indian police force. However, he said I had to decide for myself and Mum remained neutral. I decided to give it a go after further thought on the basis that if it all went terribly wrong I still had my trade and could always return to that. I now had to tell my employers at 'Longleys' – not something I was looking forward to. Nobody from the firm tried to dissuade me and my contract manager at the time Mr Carter said that if things did not work out then I would always be welcomed back. I really appreciated that.

My start date in the police was advised to me and I duly turned up not knowing exactly what to expect. During the first few days I was fitted out with two uniforms including one black and one white helmet (for Summer use), together with all other items needed by a police officer. Brighton was the only force in the country to wear white helmets and in my opinion it was a sad day when years later it stopped. I had already been told that I would be required to attend police training college in Kent for a period of 5 months, but as the new course didn't start until 4 weeks later I was assigned to the new headquarters maintenance man. I was not impressed. I had not joined to sell my trade knowledge on the cheap, and I soon realised I knew far more than the man I was supposed to be assisting. The impatience of youth!

Time went by and I was soon on my way to Sandgate in Kent to be immersed and trained in the ways of the British police. Everything about the course was carried out under a strict regime where anyone who stepped out of line soon got jumped on. However, I had been an apprentice working under such conditions, so it made no difference to me and I adapted very easily. Our section had some very appropriate names in its line-up which included me, 'Constable', a 'Sargent' and a 'Copper' and when we were assembled on parade we had to shout out our names and force. It never failed to raise a giggle in the ranks. Most of the time was spent in the classroom learning different aspects of police law which I found very interesting and different and I still remember a lot of what I learnt from the police 'Bible' that went by the name of 'Moriarty's Police Law Book'. We were supervised and drilled throughout our stay at Sandgate by an amazing person by the name of Sergeant Squires. As he was a member of the Kent police force he didn't have to comply with the height requirement of 6ft. He was about 5ft 6in and about just as wide, but as smart as anyone and bolt upright in stature. Part of Sergeant Squires duties was to perfect our marching, ready for the passing out parade on completion of the course which took place in front of local dignitaries and invited guests and included close family. Any mistakes were punished in several ways put forward by our sergeant, when the offender could choose his punishment. The options were:

1. March to the bottom of the steep hill leading into the centre and crouch down like a frog and hop up to the top of the hill.

2. Pay a fee to Sergeant Squires' charity for local sick children.

The first was incredibly painful and most people paid up. I made sure I got all the moves correct until the final practice before the passing out when, instead of shooting my head to the right when called upon, I for some reason looked left and decided to hop up the hill. Oh, the pain! I wished I had chosen 'option 2'.

Feeding so many young officers was a problem in itself, most were strapping men who ate a large quantity of food, which we got, but the quality needed much to be desired. Fridays was fish and chip day for the evening meal and was considered the best meal of the week until one of my fellow officers found a cigarette in amongst his chips. I don't know what action was taken but the food did improve somewhat after.

Police on parade, with 'Sargent' (far right), 'Copper' (second right) and myself, 'Constable'.

Our fitness was taken very seriously by the physical training officer who went by the name of 'Punchy Wallace' – as his background was as a British lightweight boxing champion, or at least that was his story. Punchy was about 5ft 6in, short for a police officer, with a face that looked like it had taken a battering at some point. He was as hard as nails with a temper to cause an earthquake. Everybody tried to keep on the right side of him until he came up against a gentle giant by the name of Terry Dugdale, a student officer from Eastbourne. Terry was a big boy and when I say big I mean big and strong as an ox, he would have made at least two of me and most of the others on the course. Punchy was determined to show off his skills and drive home his reputation at self-defence and his mode of attack. At one of the first sessions he thought he was going to make his point by picking on the biggest student in the class when he called Terry forward to the centre of our group. "When I give you the word you attack me", shouted Punchy. Our Terry didn't wait for the end of the sentence when he lunged forward with Punchy still having his hands down at his side and grabbed him with his arms right around the outside of him. Our beloved leader's face got redder and redder, and the more he tried to get free the tighter Terry pulled his grip. Terry was having none of it, he had been told to attack and attack he had and without any intentions of letting go. The rest of the group was starting to look worried as by this time Punchy was starting to struggle to get his breath when Terry decided to let the poor man go. Bad decision. As soon as he was free, Punchy sprang into action and within a split-second Terry was on his back with his arms pinned down and locked behind his back. It was at this point that Punchy started to get very violent and started to pummel Terry from all sides and then started to bang his head against the wooden floor. It all came to an end when Punchy decided he had made his point and he let Terry get up, at the same time giving the following advice to all the class: "Don't forget boys, when you have immobilized your man with a good beating and before you let him free or have the handcuffs on, never under any circumstances let go of him". A lesson that I have remembered to this day. There was no political correctness or rules that couldn't be overlooked in those days and we had learnt a big lesson which I carried with me for the rest of my working life. Once you have someone on the ropes mentally as well as physically don't let them get back in the fight, it's a good tip for any businessman.

Strange as it may seem, Punchy took a liking to me in so far as he had this strange idea I could play football. The only reason I can think why, was that I played, not that well, quite a lot during our keep fit classes. When I returned to the Brighton force at the end of the training I was approached by two older officers who requested that I play in the next game being played by the force on the following Wednesday. I tried to explain that they must have made some kind of mistake as I was hopeless at playing football and always had been. They told me it wasn't what my training report said, in fact I had come highly recommended by Punchy. I had thought he was totally mad from the very beginning, now I knew he was. Did I ever play football for Brighton police? Well yes actually I did, just the once and was never invited to do so ever again. I did try to explain to the manager that there must be some sort of mistake, but he wasn't having it. During our training we all became very fit under the guidance of Sergeant Wallace, who always insisted that it was necessary to go on a 5 mile run along Sandgate seafront just before all of us were released for the rest of the weekend at Saturday lunch time. Punchy was not one for taking part in any of the activities himself so he just drove up and down the seafront bellowing out of his car window the most awful blasphemous language to drive us on at a greater speed. He knew that everyone was just busting to get away to have a bit of time to themselves after a gruelling week. He was a raving schizophrenic, we were all convinced of that. He put us through this performance every week for the whole of the course and achieved his goal of getting us all fit.

As the course drew to a close with our minds stuffed full of police regulations and law, and as fit as whippets, it was time for our passing out parade. The parade consisted of speeches from the local mayor and the course commandant followed by us lot carrying out a series of synchronised marching displays.

During the hours that we were made to practice, Sergeant Squires would rave throughout at anyone who got anything wrong, to the point his face would turn bright red and we thought he was going to have a heart attack (I heard a few years later that he did indeed die of just that). The language he used to express his feelings was pretty rich and would often turn the air blue, this affected some of the less worldly recruits who just went to pieces and made even more mistakes. Limb co-ordination was not a strong point for some. All this shouting and bad language didn't affect me at all, my working class and building background stood me in good stead, I found it all very amusing.

On completion we all returned to our own forces when the real job began. It seemed very strange to be out on the streets of Brighton in uniform and the general public relying on you in so many ways. Working shift hours around the clock was not something I had given a great deal of thought to and at first it affected me greatly. I never really got used to it. There were a few occasions I even fell fast asleep, standing up, on night duty in shop doorways. I was assigned to 'A' division which covered many of the hot spots of Western Road, North Street, South Street and all areas in between which made me adapt to the unseemly side of a police officer's life. Very early on I came across a local thug by the name of John Henry Jones (not

The passing out parade that heralded the beginning of my career in the Brighton police force (I am circled in the photograph).

his real name, I'm no mug). He may be a 100 years old by now but I'm not going to take a chance on him reading this. He would try to intimidate me by keeping his hand inside the breast pocket of his jacket to make me think he was carrying a weapon. Of course, the more experienced officers took no notice but to us new boys it could be very frightening.

It wasn't all doom and gloom as there were many amusing and light-hearted moments and I find them just as funny now as I did when they first happened. In the early hours of one morning I got a call saying that a member of the public had reported that a neighbour in an adjoining flat had not been seen for several days. Deliveries of milk were accumulating on the door step and the front door was slightly open and also the person who was reporting this could hear a hissing sound coming from inside the flat. I was to investigate. Off I went and met up with the person who had reported the incident, after a quick check I decided I had better enter and see what was going on. In front of me was a long hallway with doors on either side. I tried the light switch but nothing happened, then I opened the first door and shone my torch around finding nothing and nobody. On I went, opening all the doors and finding nothing until I came to the end of the hall when I looked up and saw a figure looking straight back at me. I froze, only to suddenly realise that I was looking in a full length mirror at myself. By now beads of sweat were forming on my face. I gently turned the handle of the last door but soon found that something was preventing it from opening on the other side and then noticed that the reported hissing sound had got louder as I had walked along the hall. By this time I had convinced myself that I had a dead body on the other side of the door and probably a suicide. What to do? I decided that I had to get into the room so stepped back and did a sort of charge at the door with my shoulder. The door gave way and I shot into the room like a rocket. I couldn't make out what was in front of me as the room was in complete darkness, apart from my torch which had dropped from my grip as I had charged in. I managed to find the light switch and turned on the light when at the same time two faces popped out from above the bed sheets. "Police" I said, not knowing what else to say. "What's going on? There is a report from your neighbour of a problem here, get out of the bed with your hands out in front of you". This the couple did without any hesitation, even though they were both stark naked. I could see I had stumbled into something that I had no jurisdiction over and removed myself from the room requesting that they get dressed. I felt a complete idiot but kept up my pretence of it being a serious incident by getting out my pocket book and taking their names and addresses etc. which revealed they were close neighbours – both married but not to each other. I then went on to explain the offence of wasting police time, which was totally irrelevant but sounded very official, and that leaving the front door open and milk on the doorstep was asking for trouble and a risk to their own security. I couldn't get away quick enough. I had a strong suspicion, and have often wondered, if the whole episode had been set up by the couple's other halves, but we shall never know the full story, shall we?

I spent a great deal of my time as a beat officer pounding the streets. Such a good way of policing as it linked the general public closely with the local officers and had far better results than today's distance policing. I also spent a lot of time with what was then known as 'The Heavy Mob'. This consisted of about eight officers led by an inspector or a sergeant who cruised the town looking for trouble, or to be ready to respond to any fights and general disorder that may break out, mainly due to excessive drinking at weekends. Fighting and violence was never one of my strong points and until my police time I had always managed to avoid it, but I soon got into the swing of things.

The early part of the 1960s was a period of two groups of young people called Mods and Rockers. The Mods rode scooters and the Rockers rode motorbikes. Both groups had a distinctive dress code. Mods wore modern clothes with jackets which had a thick fur collar, while Rockers wore black leather. Brighton was one of the meeting places of these two groups, mainly at weekends when pitched battles would take place along the seafront. Our job was to deal with this public disorder and enforce the law. All leave would be cancelled at weekends when we would gather in our groups ready to respond to any outbreak of violence which, whilst difficult, produced some memorable incidents.

In my group we had an officer who was ex Royal Navy and built like a destroyer and was one; a destroyer, I mean, of the opposition, fists like a blacksmith's hammer and as strong as an ox. I kept close to 'Sailor', what other name would we call him? One Rocker decided he would take him on and refused to move when he was told to do so. Words were exchanged before the

Rocker produced a bike chain, a weapon often used. I was close to him when Sailor with one swift move hit the young Rocker square on the chin with dramatic effect: his chin departed from his jaw bone and dropped down on his chest. Before he was carted off to hospital, the ambulance crew had to tie the rocker's chin to the top of his head before they could move him, we heard no more of the incident.

On another occasion I was on duty at the Clock Tower, soon after I had returned from Sandgate, when a member of the public came running up to my partner and me (we always patrolled in pairs in the centre of Brighton) screaming out that a fight had broken out in 'The Quadrant Pub' in Queen's Road. Off we went, people were fighting outside and inside the place and all hell had broken loose. It felt like us two against the world, and I was expected to join in. My partner, who was an experienced officer, drew his truncheon so I thought I had better do the same and in we went. Bottles and glasses were flying everywhere, punches being thrown and all in all general chaos. I had no idea what I was going to do so just kept very, very, close to my partner. Self-preservation was definitely on my mind. We got to the bar where the bar staff were taking refuge. I saw my colleague make a bee line for one of those who was in the centre of the melee, with his back to us, and grab him by the hair and yank him backwards and dragging him by the hair towards the entrance door. I grabbed him by the collar of his jacket and between us we managed to get him outside. Still dragging him, we got the man to the police box where we dispatched him inside with some force. He hit the back of the box and went down. After we had called up the station and he had been picked up I asked my partner how he knew which man to grab. "No idea", was the reply "I just wanted to get anyone, to show we meant business and to cool the whole thing down". Which of course it did. I don't think that would have gone down in today's society, but oh so effective.

Another time we were all sitting around at the station one bank holiday waiting to be called out to another invasion by the Mods and Rockers. The call went up that fighting had started between the two groups on the seafront just by the Palace Pier. All of our helmets and truncheons were lined up ready for us to grab on our way out to the transport. Off we go again I thought, grabbed my stuff and we were soon on our way when I noticed our sergeant was brandishing a wooden crib board in his hand. It turned out that he couldn't find his truncheon so he had grabbed the nearest thing available. The undying memory I have of the whole incident was of seeing our sergeant chasing a crowd of yobs along the seafront with the crib board raised above his head in the most unthreatening manner. After almost two years I came to the conclusion that the police force was not for me: shift work, unsocial hours, working weekends and of course what I saw as always having to put myself in harm's way for a poor wage. I had known from the outset about some of these things but until I had tried, I didn't appreciate how it would affect me. No excuses, I had made a mistake, but it was an experience that I learnt a lot from and has helped me in many ways since, not least of not being such a wimp.

Chapter 7
Planning our Married Life

During my time in the police force I met the person who has had the greatest influence on my life. It all started with a bet with my friend Ivan when we were attending a Saturday night at the Regent Ballroom, which once stood near the Clock Tower, where part of Boots the chemist now stands. We were walking around the ballroom eyeing up the girls when I spotted the most beautiful girl. I couldn't take my eyes off her. Ivan saw who I was looking at and decided to ask her to dance with him, I tried to put him off by betting him sixpence that she would refuse. My idea being that he wouldn't want to risk his money. Unfortunately for me he accepted the bet. Off he went and to my amazement, without any hesitation, she accepted. Not only had I missed out but I had to pay sixpence for the privilege. Weeks passed and by this time I was going out with another girl I had met. We were invited to a party and Ivan had got an invite as well. Who did he bring? Yes, the beauty I had missed out on! Many weeks later I was at the Regent again. I was on my own following my break-up with the other girlfriend and this time luck was on my side because the beautiful Jennifer was there by herself. We got talking and that, as they say, was that. I was still in the police force at this time and didn't have much money, in fact I was completely broke and only had enough money to buy one drink. I made the excuse that I wasn't thirsty, so Jen drank on her own. How awful was that!

After dropping her at her home in Southwick, I still had my Ford Anglia car, we arranged that I would pick her up the following evening to go to the cinema to see the latest James Bond film. I had no money to buy the tickets but I had a cunning plan. The police had an agreement with all the cinema managements that they would allow all officers in free on production of their warrant card, if they were prepared to be called upon if any problem occurred with any of the other patrons during the showing of the film. Easy! We arrived at the Odeon cinema and saw that there was a long queue stretching back up West Street, but we joined the queue. I stood chatting away without a care in the world, with the stunning Jennifer holding my arm. What more could a man want? I really liked her. Eventually we got to the box office and I explained who I was and expected to be let straight in but the woman said she was sorry, but the arrangement didn't apply on Sunday evenings. I was lost for words and hadn't any money but thinking quickly and in my very authoritative policeman voice told her to get the manager who soon arrived. I remember Jen just stood there and took it all in her stride without a blink of an eye while I explained to the manager why it was in his best interest that we be let in. He soon got the picture and we were given our free tickets before we went in to see the latest James Bond film.

Weeks turned into a few months and we saw more and more of each other and I soon decided that Jen was the one person I wanted to spend the rest of my life with. The time came for me to ask her to marry me, which I did, and she accepted. I think she thought I had gone mad or was having a joke with her.

It was Jen that I turned to when I decided to leave the police as her future was going to be on the line as well as my own. Her agreement and opinion was very important for what would lay ahead for us both. It was the first big decision we made together and, like all the others since, she backed my judgement one hundred percent, never ever letting me down. I loved her from the beginning and I have loved her ever since, nobody could ever have had a better person to spend their life with.

Buying the engagement ring was a pointer to the future, it was decided that we would have a look around the jewellers in Brighton. What I didn't realise was how many there were or that we were going to visit all of them. When we looked in the first shop it was very encouraging as Jen seemed to take to one ring straight away, so I thought great this isn't going to take long, should be home for lunch. I was informed that whilst she liked it she wanted to look and compare it with other rings to make sure. Several hours later after visiting numerous jewellery shops, I lost count of the number, we returned to the first one we looked at and bought the ring. I've tried to avoid going shopping with my dear wife ever since, buying online was I'm sure invented just for me.

Before the day of our engagement it was, in those days, required of the perspective son-in-law to ask the girl's father for his permission. On my next visit to Jen's house I was encouraged to do what I had to do, by Jen and her mum disappearing out of the room leaving me with my future father-in-law. Fortunately, on me asking, he agreed straight away. Bearing in mind Jen was only 19-years-old at the time, I thought he was very brave. I would never have agreed to it with my own daughter.

Our first priority was to save as much as we could as quickly as we were able, my car had been sold and replaced with an old minivan which didn't last long before it had to be scrapped. My contribution to the pot at the beginning was almost nil. Jen had some savings and her salary was higher than mine from her job as a secretary, so she wasn't getting much of a bargain on the deal. We decided between us that our first priority was to accumulate as much money as possible to get a deposit for a mortgage in order that we could buy our own house. All my brothers, sister and friends had or were living in rented accommodation. I could never see why anyone would want to pay over most of their wages to someone else. We reasoned that at least we would have something eventually after paying off a mortgage.

As Jen worked for an estate agent we were in a position to look at properties as soon as they came onto the market – if they were in our price range. We went to see a new house which was for sale at Woodingdean just outside Brighton. Jen fell in love with it and we wanted to buy it, and that was when the problems started. We tried everything to persuade a building society to give us a mortgage, but they were very strict on who they lent to depending on what their income was, what sort of future employment prospects were, etc. We didn't qualify with anyone's criteria; the house was just too expensive for our combined income. After much searching I received a phone call from Jen to tell me that a property had become available which seemed to be in our price range, and we needed to look at it as soon as we could. We arranged to meet at the house which was 30 Waldegrave Road, not far from Preston Park in Brighton, which turned out to be a large semi-detached Victorian property. Jen produced the keys and in we went. It was a spooky atmosphere inside the house which was still full of the previous owner's furniture who, we had been told, had recently died. When we entered the dining room we could see the old lady's breakfast still on the table with the chair upon which she must have been sitting laying on its back. All had been left just as she had exited the world and the front door afterwards. Strangely enough none of this put us off at all. On having a good look around and noting what we thought needed doing to get it in good order we decided to try to buy it, but of course it was never going to be that easy. The asking price was £3,000 but we were advised by Jen's boss to offer an extra £50 which he said would secure a deal, which it did. Again, obtaining a mortgage was proving to be difficult but on the advice of the solicitor, Mr White, who we had been introduced to us by Jen's boss, we eventually got fixed up with 'The Brighton and Southern Counties Building Society'. We still had to pay a slightly higher interest rate than was normal because we were considered a higher risk and only then because my father-in-law stood as a guarantor that he would pay the mortgage if we failed to do so.

Prior to us obtaining the house when I had been working on my own, I received a letter right out of the blue from Longley's, my old employer, at James Longley & Co in which their contract manager Tom Carter said, "We understand that you have now got the police force idea out of your system, when are you coming back to us?". Well, you could have knocked me over with a feather. To think that they had kept tabs on me, held no bad feelings, and must have thought highly enough of me to want me back.

I soon made contact and was offered a job back at my trade on the construction of a new house for Mr Norman Longley's brother, Basil, at West Chiltington. I didn't know it then, but it was to open up a whole new world to me. When this project was complete I was approached to see if I would be interested in taking a position as a carpenter foreman under the management group headed by a young manager by the name of Micheal Biles. The only problem with this position was that it was to build new premises for a food retailer called 'Nurdin and Peacock' in Watford. Jen and I discussed it as we would only see each other at weekends, but it was too good an offer to turn down. The money was very good, and it was a step on the promotion ladder, so I took the job. Part of the package was that I would receive a living allowance to pay for my accommodation, a food allowance and also to receive all the travelling costs that I incurred. The trick was to get all these extras without spending all of it, or in my case any of it. One other person also joined our team to be the 'ganger man' who was to supervise all the labourers. He was a slightly built man called Pat Doughty, a fiercely Irish republican who loved to sing republican songs of hate of the British. I got on with him very well, when he was sober. It was a real mixed management team on site with the senior man being a Scot by the name of Jock McLevy who again was a fierce republican. When we eventually arrived on the site Pat and I had to spend time looking for somewhere to live and finished up local to the site living with this weird Italian woman and her even stranger husband from north Africa. The arrangement wasn't great as most of the living allowance was being handed over to our hosts and that was not my idea at all, so I came up with an alternative: why not provide our own sleeping quarters? I ordered an additional storage shed for the site and soon had it erected, waterproofed and fitted out with homemade beds and purchased some cooking facilities. We already had washing and cleaning arranged for the workers on site so we could use those, and we were soon ready to move in. Pat the ganger man had agreed to move in with me, so I promptly put him in charge of cooking and cleaning. From this moment on all the money from my living allowance was added to our savings for our new home. Pat would go off some nights and not come back for a couple of days, I don't know where he went but I do know he wasn't faithful to his wife. I just kept myself to myself and kept saving.

We decided to get married on September 16ᵗʰ 1967 with Jen's mum and dad insisting that they would pay for the reception and Jen's wedding dress. This was to our great relief as we needed every penny we could get to pay for the house and its modernisation. We saved every last penny we could, going to all sorts of lengths not to spend money even on what could be said as essential things. When holes appeared in my only pair of wearable shoes I refused to have them mended, so I cut thick cardboard and lined the inside. This was fine until it rained, and the card disintegrated.

As I write this account of my life in 2018, the news is all about young people not being able to get on to the housing ladder and what they can't afford. Anyone born in the last 45 years has no idea how hard it was for our generation. Some even have the temerity to suggest that what we worked for over so many years was come by too easily and in some way should be taken away. Over my dead body. Unfortunately, or fortunately, our generation have made it our life's work to improve things for the present generation so that they don't have to experience the hardships that we and our forebears had to endure when we were young. Our children and

Jen and I on our wedding day, September 16th 1967, St Michael's Church, Southwick.

grandchildren can't know what hardship is. That's not to say that some young people don't, the great majority have warm clothes, don't go hungry, and have a roof over their heads

As I was working away all the week, the work on the house slowed but we both set to at weekends and worked very hard to get it into shape. My Dad helped me take the wall down between two rooms and to install a steel beam to form a large through lounge. While we were in the middle of doing this a lorry loaded with bricks that I had ordered turned up which needed to be unloaded, we stopped what we were doing and went out to help the driver unload. Soon after we had started, Jen came out with her gloves on and started to join in when my Dad just innocently said, "It's all right my duck, we can manage". I can't remember exactly what her reply was, but it was straight and to the point saying that she was quite capable of unloading a few bricks. Now my Dad was completely taken aback by this reaction and tried to smooth things over, which he did, but it was the first I saw of the iron determination my future wife had of doing anything she wanted to do. I still shudder to this day when I think what we did to that beautiful Victorian house. We decided to modernise it, the stupidity of the young. Out came the ornamental plaster cornices, walls were taken down, new modern windows in the rear kitchen, new modern glazed front door and I made all new kitchen cabinets and a seating area all in the 60s style. I hang my head in shame, we even had bright orange wallpaper and carpets! Choosing the wallpaper was a difficult moment as we couldn't agree on anything and just settled with a match for the carpet. We have never again had wallpaper in any house we have lived in for over 50 years, and this also applies to toilet roll holders.

We couldn't afford to furnish our new house or finish the work on it before we were married but we got it to a position where we could live in it. Jen's mum and dad bought us a bed for a wedding present and I did a deal with my brother Terence for his old three-piece suite, for which I gave him £5 and a roof rack.

Our great day came and we were married on September 16th 1967 at St Michael's Church, Southwick, near to where Jen's parents lived. The priest who performed the ceremony was

The newly weds, Jen and I at a party in 1968.

the Reverend Levy who left us with a repeated discussion topic between us right up until this day. Prior to the wedding we were asked to attend a meeting with the Reverend when he discussed with us what we should expect from our marriage, most of which is long forgotten. Our marriage has always been of complete equality, believe me Jen would not accept anything else and to be fair to myself nor would I. However, the Reverend did give me one advantage when he told us that if any disagreement ever arose that we could not resolve then me, as the man and head of the household, should make any final decision and my opinion should take preference in any resolution. I'm not sure what tablets the Rev was on and I don't think he was insane, but I knew his instructions were doomed to failure. Jen is the most single-minded person, except for her dad, I have ever known. Telling her what she was or was not going to do has proved to be laughable. If we don't agree on anything then we just don't do it at all or talk until we reach a compromise, it seems to have worked.

After our wedding I told my employer that I wouldn't stay working away from home anymore and was transferred to a new site at Sussex University where my Dad was working. After I had been there for a few days, I was informed my Dad had had an accident and told to urgently get down to one of the rooms on the ground floor. When I got to the room I found my Dad at the bottom of a deep manhole with the rescue services trying to extricate him from the depths of the hole. All I can see now is my poor Dad's face looking up at me from about 6 metres below with severe pain etched all over his face. When he was eventually hauled out he was rushed to hospital for an emergency operation. He had broken his femur in two places as well as his lower leg. When I went back to look at the place where the accident took place I could see just how lucky he had been not to have been killed. The small hole he had fallen through had guided him straight down missing all the metal foot holds that were protruding from each side, if his head had hit just one it would have killed him. He spent many weeks in hospital with his leg in traction and, even with all the attention he received, he finished up with one leg shorter than the other, having to wear a special built up shoe to compensate. Dad never fully recovered.

≈ * ≈

Chapter 8
Climbing the Ladder

Once the house at 30 Waldegrave Road was completed, Jen decided she didn't like living in Brighton. By this time we were expecting our first child, so we decided to sell the house. We looked far and wide in mid Sussex in the search for our next home and found ourselves driving through Hurstpierpoint. We came across a new development nearing completion on what had been known as the Chinese Gardens. We had a look around the semi-detached show house and were very impressed. When we were just about to leave we were informed that there was one detached house left just around the corner. Not knowing if we could afford it we went to have a look, instantly liked it and promptly reserved it. As has always been normal for us we had a great deal of aggravation selling the house in Brighton to several potential buyers. Finally, we secured a sale for £3,750 – an increase of £700. After deducting the cost of modernisation we were on our way to making our first profit on property.

It was at this time that I was transferred to the next construction site which was at Surrey University in Guildford and given a section to supervise known as the Great Hall with its adjacent restaurant. I was still paid by the hour which meant that I could be dismissed without notice, no sick pay and none of the benefits received like a full member of staff. I had been given an old company car which was a Morris Oxford, previously used with 120,000 miles on the clock, by my old contract manager Tom Carter, it really was a wreck. We made good use of it for some months and even went on holiday in it. I was on my way home from work one evening when I felt something strange with the steering, out I got only to find one of the tyres was punctured. After having worked out where the spare wheel was and got the jack in position I started to turn the handle to raise the car up. As the pin, set in the underside, was rising it was pushing up into the door itself and gradually collapsing the side of the car onto the ground. The whole side of the car was full of rust.

The Morris was replaced with a newer smaller Austin 1100, which was a big step up, and I was quite satisfied with my lot until out of the blue I was summoned to the main site office by one of the senior managers, Neil Covey. When I arrived and had been called into this person's office I could see by the look on his face that it was not good news. "What would you say if I told you that we are going to take away your car?", he said. A bit of a strange question to ask someone like me, and I could feel the hairs on the back of my neck rising and blood starting to rise. My answer was immediate and without hesitation, "You can arrange for my cards and money to be ready for my collection at the end of the week, so you can take this as my notice to leave". This was one of the most pivotal moments in my career. Neil Covey knew I had the better of him. Not for how good I was but that he knew who my Dad was and that I knew that his uncle was the very same Mr Bill Sheppard who was my Dad's old boss and had arranged with Mr Norman Longley that I should be given my apprenticeship years before. It's not always what you know, it's sometimes who you know. After a few days I was again told to report to Neil Covey, who on seeing me for a second time was transformed into my new best friend. I was offered full membership of the Longley staff with all the benefits: pension rights, fixed salary, paid overtime after 44 hours, sick pay – and I kept the car.

We completed the sale of Waldegrave Road and the purchase of 9 Chestnut Grove, Hurst-pierpoint, for £5,050. This was reduced by £50 because we didn't want a fireplace fitted. As it turned out, the £50 was also taken off by our solicitor but we didn't argue. Our outgoings were more than our income, as our daughter had been born and my salary was the only income we had. The moving-in day arrived and to save money we decided to move ourselves, borrowing a van from my employer. For some reason our mattress finished up tied to the top of the firm's car and it jumped and flapped up the A23.

Moving into our first and only new property felt wonderful and for me the first time living out of Brighton permanently. I loved it. We had hardly any furniture and couldn't afford to buy what was needed. I even made a dining table during overtime on a Saturday, along with anything that we needed which avoided us spending money. My Mum gave us some old chairs we had when I was a child and some similar ones from Jen's parents helped to make a set which we painted to match the table. What we couldn't afford we went without. Our three-piece suite came from a couple, that Jen's parents knew, at a knock down price, I think they felt sorry for us.

Before moving, our daughter, Emma Jane Constable, was born on June 16th 1969 in Brighton General Hospital at the top of Elm Grove. I was with Jen when Emma was born, a truly amazing moment I will never forget. I saw the top of her head just before she popped out. I have loved her from that moment and feel just the same about her now. Throughout all the ups and downs of family life I have always looked on her as mine, I wonder what her children Leo and Jessica and husband Mike will think of that? If, or when, they come to read this account.

As the new house wasn't completed when Emma was born, and I couldn't be around to look after Jen and the new baby, my in-laws let us stay with them for a few weeks. Both of them were amazing to us and that is the way it continued for the rest of their lives. Mum and Dad

Marsh were without any doubt the best in-laws anyone could have had, and I loved them as my own. I am able to say that we never had one cross word or falling out in all our married life up until they died.

At first, we found our financial position with the mortgage on the house and the new baby impossible even with me working long hours. Jen's mum knew we were struggling and what our problem was but never said a word but just decided to visit us every Monday evening, bringing bags of food along with anything else they thought was useful. It also gave them an opportunity to see their new grandchild which started a special relationship between them that lasted all their lives.

To augment our income something had to be done and Jen found the answer: by becoming an underwear saleswoman via a party system entitled 'PIPA-DEE'. What it involved was setting up parties in other peoples' houses in the evenings, at which she would sell this particular make of women's underwear to the partygoers who had been invited by the hostess. In return, the hostess would receive free underwear depending on the amount sold. Jen always was a very shy person so how she forced herself to go around the streets knocking on doors during the day with Emma in her pram trying to get other women to hold one of her parties took an awful lot of guts and determination, but that is something she has plenty of. She would arrive home late at night from a party tired and worn out, hand over everything to me and then together we would check all the orders and count up the takings before crawling into bed in the early hours.

Emma, as much as we loved her, was not an easy baby. This was not her fault as it turned out. Putting her to bed was a problem almost from the start, quite simply she didn't want to go. Night after night I would lay her down in her cot, sit on the floor holding her hand through the bars in the hope that she would go to sleep. Just when I thought she had dropped off I would release my hand and edge towards the door. As soon as I was outside she would scream and shout until I returned to my position beside her and have to start the whole process over again. In the middle of the night she would wake at all sorts of hours and go through the whole performance of hand holding until she went back to sleep. If I left her she just screamed and shouted the house down until I returned. On many occasions I would just get dressed, put Emma in her carry cot and drive her around the countryside until she went to sleep aided by the movement of the car. In the end it was found that she was suffering from a form of tonsillitis but not until, in desperation, I put her pram alongside our bed and pushed and rocked it with one leg out of the bed in order to save my sanity and get some sleep myself.

In 1970 I met a couple who were to become our lifelong friends. I had just started work on a new project in Durrington, near Worthing, for the Temperance Building Society as an assistant manager to an old friend of my Dad's, Terry Hearn. At the same time that I joined the team a new engineer had just been appointed by the name of Brian Finch. Brian and his wife Brenda, along with their little girl Clare, had just moved into the area from London. I have never been able to live down one story that Brian reminds me of as often as he can. One section of the project that I was managing was a new swimming pool which had to be tested under strict conditions to ensure it didn't leak. Parts of the testing involved checking the water level at regular intervals on a gauge set across on a corner of the pool. A green dye had to be added to the water so if it leaked out it would be obvious to spot. On completion of the concrete structure the gauge was set in position and the level of the water checked by the engineer's representative to ensure the accuracy for each weekly check. I thought I should keep a special watch on how things were holding up so after 2 or 3 days I checked the water level when, to my horror, I could see that it had fallen slightly. I put this down to the initial absorption into the concrete structure and the hot weather we were experiencing. I let several days pass before the official check was to be made again only to find the water table was down again. What to do? I couldn't let the whole structure fail on the first test. I came to the decision that I should get to site before anyone arrived the next morning and top up the water level. This I did, and the test was passed. I also had to do the same thing on several more occasions until one day I was walking over to the pool when I saw Terry Hearn walking towards me flanked by two very official looking men. I was introduced by Terry and then asked the very revealing question, "Are you using a green dye to test your swimming pool?". To which I had to reply that I was. "Ah!" said one of our visitors, "we've found the source". It turned out that the water in the river some several miles away had turned green and the two men were from the river authorities. Doing some quick thinking I explained that we had indeed had a leak and that also a quantity of the dye had been spilt which I suspected had caused the problem. After further discussions it was agreed we would empty the pool and carry out repairs before any further testing and fortunately that was the last we heard of it. Explaining all this to the checking engineer was a little more difficult, but when he heard about the spillage and I had explained that I had noticed a sudden drop in the water level and was emptying the pool to check the reason, all was back on course.

Brian and Brenda became our very good friends and we went on numerous holidays together. They went on to have a son Andrew and another daughter Johanna, their eldest Clare and Andrew being the same age as our two children. So many incidents occurred on our holidays together that it would fill another book on its own, so I will only record a few. The first one was on our holiday to a place called Brean Sands in Somerset. Neither of us had much money but we both had company cars so all we had to find was sufficient money to pay for our accommodation. After much consideration we decided on a cheap property where we would be able to cook for ourselves. After a long drive and search we came across the property. I remember sitting in the car thinking this just can't be it, it didn't begin to resemble the property that was in the brochure. I was all for turning around and going straight home and had to be encouraged to get out of the car to go inside. The outside was bad, but the inside was even worse. After much discussion we decided to stay but to clean the place up, with the babies sleeping in their prams rather than taking a risk on the cleanliness of the cots. Another lesson learnt, never go for the cheapest option. If anything looks too good to be true it probably is. This experience never put us off and we went on many other holidays together.

Another story was the time we were on a canal boat when, in my usual courteous way, I constantly reminded the children not to get near the edge and fall in the water. To be fair I did go on about it a lot but I was concerned with their safety. On the final day I was hanging over the side when we were trying to navigate a tight bend. I slipped and went straight in the water. Everyone saw the funny side except me who was spluttering and coughing all over the place, clinging to the side of the boat and being dragged along. Needless to say I have never been allowed to forget what happened.

On holiday with the Finches in the 1980s.

Another time we were on a river boat holiday in France, when the children were not with us, and we turned up at a small village late in the evening. We looked around in the hope that we would find somewhere to eat but everything was closed up. Just when we were about to give up we spotted a lady working in her garden, so we went over to ask her if she knew anywhere we could get a meal. "Just a moment" she said, and went off into her house. When she returned she informed us that she had phoned the restaurant in the adjoining village to see if they could accommodate us, and they could so she had booked us a table. Our only problem was that we had no means of getting to where we needed to go and explained this to the women. Back in the house she went and then came back to tell us that her husband was going to take us. We got in his car and went on a 20-minute ride to the restaurant. When we arrived, we were greeted by the proprietor who took us through the restaurant to a back room, which was full of all the locals having their evening meal and chatting. We were served the most delicious meal before asking our host if he would be able to call us a taxi, to which he replied that all was arranged and took us back to our boat. Before we left, we bought a couple of bottles of the wine we had been drinking and left them outside the house of the couple who had been so kind to us.

As with all the houses we have lived in it wasn't long before we needed more room, so we decided to extend and improve the new house. Our friend Brian produced the drawings and obtained planning permission on our behalf for a single-story extension to include a new dining room. The plan was also to turn the area between the house and the garage into a new entrance hall, with the existing front door being moved so as to accommodate a new cloakroom. Brian's architectural skills came in very handy for many years to come.

I gained further promotion at work and took charge of my first site completely on my own – a new office block in the centre of Kingston-upon-Thames for the Provincial Building Society which turned out to be a baptism of fire. The project was for a five-floor block of offices over a basement, with a lift in one corner going down into the basement. The lift became very significant in what happened shortly after the commencement of the project. I was given a set of the architects' and engineers' drawings and told to get on with the job. The architects were a practice by the name of 'Hardesty and Partners', with Geoff Hardesty being the partner in charge, and the engineers were 'Scott White and Hookings'. I only remember the engineer's name as Peter, a really nice person about the same age as me. I set out the site, we had to do everything ourselves in those days, and we started to excavate the basement. A few days passed when there was a knock on the site office door and on opening it I was greeted by an elderly gentleman who introduced himself as the site's next door neighbour. He happened to be a solicitor and seemed to be very helpful and cooperative and enquired when I would be carrying out the internal survey to his property. This survey was to record its condition in case of any problems occurred in the future. When we had agreed an appointment for me to carry out the survey he asked if it would be possible for a carpenter to adjust his front door as it was difficult to open, so in the interest of being a good neighbour I readily agreed and off he went. I had a word with Ken the carpenter and sent him along to sort out the door problem, after which he confirmed back to me that the difficulty had been sorted. About 2 hours later back came my new friend, the solicitor, saying that he was sorry to trouble me but the door was still causing a problem. In fact, it seemed worse. "That's strange", I said "the carpenter said he had fixed it, I'll send him around straight away". On confronting Ken, he said that he had indeed fixed the door and couldn't see how it was still causing a problem. I sent him along anyway to check and on his return he reported to me that it was all a bit strange as he could hardly open the door and had had to force it. It was then that the penny dropped like a heavy weight and my heart went to my boots. We were excavating the base to the lift in the corner of the site next to the entrance door of our man's property. I shot out of the office to where the excavations were taking place and sure enough my worst fears were confirmed. The building next door was falling into my site. As the site was near to the river Thames, water was pouring out from under the adjacent building washing away its foundations and the digger driver was either too thick or stupid to see what was happening. I immediately stopped the driver from what he was doing and got him filling the hole back in again. I had rescued us from a complete catastrophe.

I contacted our head office and spoke to one of our directors who was an engineer and he came out to see me straight away. In the meantime, I contacted our scaffolding company who arrived within a couple of hours fully geared up to shore up the building next door. This they did during the evening and into the night. I stopped on site all that night and all the next day before arriving home after about 30 hours, falling in to bed completely shattered. It took me a long time to get to sleep and when I did all I could dream of was running water. After some difficult negotiations it was decided not to take the lift down into the basement and, instead, to terminate it on the ground floor. I could think of nothing else but that I had blown my chance of being my own man and running sites in my own right. As it happened, nothing more was said. In fact everyone sympathised with my situation and was most helpful, I had survived by the skin of my teeth. The potential disaster was not the only testing experience I had on the site. One of the essential jobs on any reinforced concrete structure is to ensure that all of the steel reinforcing rods which are an integral part of the work are positioned accurately and securely. I had already experienced some difficulty with the sub-contractor company who were installing the reinforcement to the fourth-floor concrete floor area, so I was double checking to ensure that everything was in the right place and fixed correctly. On this occasion, I found that there were many errors with the positioning of the steel and pointed this out to one of the operatives before contacting the foreman. Not a cleaver thing to do as I was about to find out. I was taken completely by surprise when this bull of a man came at me, head down, arms flying in all directions. I tried to move out of his way but obviously not fast enough as he hit me square in the chest and pinned me over the scaffolding safety rail by my throat. I was being choked and could hardly breath. While all this was going on I could hear the voice of my contract manager Adrian Mamby (the name says it all) shouting up from the ground floor, "Are you alright up there?". No, I thought, I enjoy being beaten up, what a !!! I was saved by the foreman of the sub-contractor who arrived with several of his men to pull the beast off of me. I gave the firm an ultimatum. Remove the attacker from site or have their contract cancelled, he was gone in minutes. The lesson to be learnt from this is to never deal with any operatives of a sub-contractor directly, always give instructions to their supervisor. They know the consequences of attacking the site manager.

They say that bad news comes in threes and so it was on my first project in charge. Jen and I were visiting my Mum and Dad one Saturday and had just got in the car to go home. We turned the radio on when there was an announcement broadcast under 'Traffic News'. It said that an accident with a lorry had occurred in the centre of Kingston-upon-Thames. The lorry had hit a scaffold surrounding a site and this had collapsed on to the adjacent main road and the emergency services were attending. I knew straight away what scaffold it was. Off we went home and then on I went to Kingston. When I arrived at the site the scaffolding company were already there, and everything was more or less back to normal. It turned out that the lorry had been loaded with the sides of its cargo overhanging the sides by a substantial amount and constituted an unsafe load. My positioning of the scaffold was checked out and found to be in accordance with the health and safety regulations. Once more, I breathed again. The rest of the construction work progressed to its conclusion, was completed within the time scale set down in the contract and had made a good profit for the firm.

It was during the time I spent on the Kingston site that our son, Mathew, was born on May 16th 1972 and again I was lucky enough to be at his birth. As soon as I saw him I could see that he didn't resemble his sister one bit, and so it turned out in many ways, some good some not so good.

Chapter 9
Bigger and Better

My next project was a new supermarket and associated buildings, including a Red Cross centre for the Sainsbury supermarket chain in East Grinstead. It was to be the largest development we had carried out for Sainsbury's, and when it was completed it had the highest takings in its first weeks of all of their new stores.

My dislike for architects in general, with a few exceptions, started on this project. The architect we were saddled with was the most dislikeable, unfriendly self-opinionated creep I ever met during my whole career – and believe me that is saying something when I think of some of them. This particular person just didn't want to contribute to the idea that I wanted to follow, of trying to work as a team, which was I thought significantly better than working against each other. At every turn he tried to find fault and criticise and to show the site team in a bad light. In so doing he was trying to show the Sainsbury staff just how clever he was. One of the good things was that Sainsbury's appointed a member of staff, who I had to deal with on a daily basis, was very helpful and did point out to me that the person in question caused problems wherever he went. To get my new-found friend onto my side I decided to take him as a guest to a cup game at the football team I have always supported, Brighton and Hove Albion. Brighton had been drawn against the non-league side Walton and Hersham at the old 'Goldstone' ground so I was expecting us to score plenty of goals on our way to the next round. I had laid on seats in the stand and some food etc. and tried to make it an entertaining afternoon. Not for the first time my team let me down as the opposition took us apart with a score of 0-4. I hoped this was not going to be how the job progressed.

The men on site named our architect 'Dr Death' because of his attitude towards them and I learnt a great deal about human nature both of our people and the pain himself. The project really stretched me to my limits in every way, mainly due to the short contract period we had signed up to and trying to keep everything moving in the right direction in spite of the lack of co-operation from Sainsbury's. I went on to build for most of the large supermarket chains including Tesco and Waitrose, along with some of the smaller outfits, all of them far superior with Waitrose coming out on top by miles.

Trying to get the project one hundred percent completed proved very difficult mainly due to the lack of information from the architects. Most of it was a small amount of decorating to external doors, but my goodness did we try by working around the clock in the final few weeks. Sainsbury's had set an opening day for the new Red Cross centre, which was not part of the contract, before our official completion which I just went along with in the hope that we would be treated fairly. Not too much to ask? At the event I was confronted by Dr Death when he accused me of not putting in enough effort to ensure the project was completed, i.e. the odd unpainted doors. I stood and listened to what he had say, I knew what he was after. He didn't want to issue the contract completion certificate which would have released a large sum of money to us. I led him to one side where I explained to him what I thought of him and that in my opinion he was going to have to answer questions on the issue of late information to us throughout the works. At the outset of the contract I had issued a list of release dates by which information needed to be issued in order for the completion date to be met and then at each monthly meeting updated it to show the actual dates when we had received it. All this was standard procedure to me and the firm. The certificate was issued and we were paid, and Jen and I never shopped at Sainsburys for the next 30 years. I never missed an opportunity to tell everyone and anyone I could what I thought of the supermarket chain. This may seem a very small gesture but as I have pointed out before forgiving and forgetting is not one of my strong subjects and as Tesco's slogan says 'every little helps'.

Once again, I was on the move as I was summoned to head office by my boss – the amazing Ray Perkins. Ray was our managing director (CEO) and he was the most unassuming quiet man you could meet. He had an iron will to get his own way by beating all opposition with kindness and understanding, if Ray wanted something you could put money on it that he would get it. I have never met a person like him, before or since, and it's true to say that he would always see the good in anyone. I for one would have done anything for him, and so would any of the company's staff.

When I arrived at his office he sat me down and explained that he wanted me to join a team to build a new shopping centre in Eastbourne. My first thoughts were that it was a long way to drive to and from each day and secondly that being part of a team was a backward step for me. I wanted to be my own man as near the top as I could get. I explained these points to Ray but as normal he was way ahead of the game and me, "Well that's a shame as it involves you getting a new car to the specification of your choice, a substantial pay increase and a sum of money each month to cover all the additional travelling you would be doing". He had me again. Later I discovered the term used to retain someone you wanted to keep as 'putting on the golden handcuffs'.

A few weeks later I visited the new site in my spanking new Austin Maxi with all the latest attachments and met up with the contract manager Michael Biles, the very same Michael that

I had worked under at the Temperance Building Society and Surrey University. The best way to describe him was as a 'loose cannon', he would answer to no-one except Ray Perkins. Michael was extremely good at his job and made a lot of money for the company, but everything had to be done his way. After about four weeks the client cancelled the project and paid the company for all their expense. We never did find out why, but we suspected that what the local authority wanted and what the client was willing to provide were two different things. The good news was that I kept my new car and increased salary but missed out on the travelling allowance. I didn't mind as I had done very well out of the situation.

During the time we were building Surrey University so many laughable things happened with Michael Biles, and for the record here is one. The story involved a haulage contractor who went by the name of Percy Podger, yes honestly it was. Percy happened to be married to a beautiful woman, Nancy Roberts, who was the hostess on a TV programme with a well-known personality of the day called Hughie Green. Michael fancied this girl and managed to convince our Percy to invite him to a special lunch given by one of the country's leading entertainment organisations at which the lady was the host. On the day of the function I had been working – making concrete test cubes to prove to the engineers that the concrete strength was to the correct level. My hands were covered in concrete when I arrived back in the office to see Michael dressed in his dinner suite trying to put his bow tie on. Without thinking, and trying to be helpful, I volunteered to help and got hold of his tie and fixed it in position without too much trouble. It wasn't until I stepped back that I saw what I had done. Poor Michael's shirt and tie were smudged all over with the remains of my concrete cubes. What to do? I decided to do nothing and was grateful that just as I had completed my task Percy's large Rolls Royce complete with driver turned up. I was able to shush Michael out of the door and into the car before he had time to look in the mirror. I thought no more about it until the end of the day just as the principal site manager, Ted Fisher, and I were about to leave for home. At that moment the Rolls Royce turned up with Michael, Percy and his wife all the worse for wear. Out they all got with Michael hardly able to stand up. After many goodbyes, thanking each other and kisses, especially between Michael and Percy's wife, off the couple went. Ted and I just wanted to go home but Michael was intent on us starting up the concrete mixer. We decided to put Michael to sleep in the First Aid room where there was a bed and let him sleep it off. After some effort and persuading we managed to get him into the First Aid room and onto the bed. Before Michael realised what was happening, Ted and I made a rush for the door with me turning the key in the lock before he could get off the bed again. After a while everything went quiet in the room and we both thought that he must have fallen asleep, so we decided that we would just leave him locked away safe and made for home. On arrival the next morning we found the door to the First Aid room was hanging from its hinges and wide open with the contents of the room completely wrecked, but no Michael. When he eventually returned to the site nothing was said and we all just carried on as if the whole episode had not occurred. Nothing was ever heard of from Percy and his wife for the remainder of the contract. Of course, there was much guesswork but Michael seemed to have gone off of Percy's wife!

After the completion of Sainsbury's the construction industry went into one of its regular downturns in work, nothing new as it has always been the first in the queue to go into recession when any problems occur in the country's economy. This is known as 'Feast or Famine' in the industry. I was sent next to a project for the Beecham Pharmaceutical company. It was a much smaller project than I had grown used to and felt that it was a backward step in my career and something I was not happy about; my ambitions were much bigger. I stuck at it for about 3 months, back to doing all my own setting out and menial tasks with very little in the way of planning and management. Eventually my impatience got the better of me. I phoned Ray Perkins and asked for a meeting and as soon as I got to see him I asked him if, by giving me a contract like he had, he was he trying to 'put me out to grass'. Ray as usual was not put out by me being so outspoken. His answer was just as direct, "Richard your future is just as important to the business as it is to you, as soon as we obtain a contract which meets what I consider is right for you then I will be in touch". That was the end of the meeting. I have suffered all my life with an extreme lack of patience, and this was one time when I thought best to keep my head down and wait. I was left in no doubt that Ray was the boss. I think I may have had a little success with the meeting because not long after Ray posted me to a project that had come to us by others misfortune. Minor work to the foundations had been started by a company by the name of 'Ronald Lyons' who had gone bankrupt. We had tendered for the work but had come second and had moved on, when the quantity surveyors for the job got in contact. The project consisted of a new headquarters for Bristow Helicopters to be built at Redhill aerodrome, complete with workshops and an enormous hanger to house the helicopters while being serviced and repaired for the oil fields in the North Sea. We inherited all of their spanking new site offices; it was obvious why they had gone bust.

My contract manager for the contract, Brian Fuller, was someone I had not worked with before and was arriving with a reputation of being a bit difficult and, shall we say, a hard task master. Brian had joined the firm about 2 years before and had brought with him a ganger man and his army of labourers, most in their mid- to late-30s and lived on the notorious Whitehawk estate in east Brighton. My new ganger man was to be Reg Gladwell. I didn't know it at the beginning but he was to turn out to be one of my greatest assets and friend, not to mention the best ganger man I ever worked with. 'Curly' Gladwell was in his mid-50s, about 5ft 8ins tall, and on the heavy side. He was kind, generous, easy to get on with, until anyone got on the wrong side of him. He would then transform into a monster with language strong even for a building site and would never hesitate to use violence if he thought it necessary. We got on just fine and I was the only person he would take orders from. I grew to love the man, but made sure we stayed on the same side, and he remained with me for the rest of his working life.

Again, I could write a separate book solely on Curly and his gang with all the funny and sometimes serious things as well, but I will have to be satisfied with recording just a few.

I was sitting in my office on site one day at lunchtime when the canteen manager, John Wyndam, came knocking at the door. As soon as I saw him I could see that something was amiss by the shock written across his face. "Come quickly", he said "there's a fight in the canteen and Curly is in the middle of it". This was the equivalent of asking me to put my head into a lion's mouth or jump out of a plane without a parachute. Firstly, I was never that brave and secondly I have never been that stupid. I explained to John that as soon as things quietened down he should come and find me when I would probably be on the other side of the aerodrome getting some fresh air. After about 10 minutes I decided to go and see what had happened and what the damage was. Inside the canteen everything was quiet with people eating lunch and reading their papers. "Everything alright in here?" I said. "Yes", said Curly "all under control". As I was about to leave I noticed that one of the scaffolders was sitting with his head in his hands and a trickle of blood running down his face, I turned and left.

I had to find out exactly what happened, so I decided to question John Wyndam and this was his account. Four people were playing cards, one of which was Curly who played a particular card (I never found out what game they were playing). For whatever reason the scaffolder called Curly a f*****g ****. "What did you call me?", says Curly. I'm not sure that the scaffolder was the sharpest knife in the drawer or, as my friends in New Zealand say, 'a sheep short in the upper paddock' but he repeated what he had said. With one swift movement Curly upended the table and hit the scaffolder straight on the nose, down he went like a sack of logs. Over the table went Curly throwing punches in all directions. It took four of his men to restrain him but not before he had got a few kicks into the scaffolder. I decided that I had to reprimand Curly in some way, so I sent for him to come to my office. He arrived after a short while and knocked on my door and came in. I asked him to sit down and said we needed to talk. After I had made a few comments about the rights and wrongs of what had happened, and him being a responsible member of my team, he gave me his reply. "Well it's like this, it's my job to get the best out of my team of labourers and keep control of them, to do this I have to have their respect or there will be mayhem". He went on to say that the moment the scaffolder swore at him he gave him the opportunity to take back what he had said and to apologise. He didn't and just repeated what he had said and had to pay the price, and he had made sure he did. I knew from then on that I needed Curly as much as he needed me, and we got on like a house on fire. All this was from a man who my children came to know as Uncle Curly and who would turn up at our house unannounced and leave Easter eggs for them on the doorstep and send them birthday cards with money in. What a wonderful man he was.

There was one other instance of a similar nature on the job which involved a labourer named Vince, not one of Curly's regular labourers. It turned out that our Vince was a local thief and that one of his side-lines was shoplifting. The cheek of the man was something else, he did his shoplifting to order from the men on site. All Vince did was collect his orders and off he would go to Marks and Spencer's, take what he wanted, and sell them on at a knock down price to those that had put in their order. I didn't know anything about this but Curly found out and decided to put a stop to it and hoped that I would be kept out of it. He confronted Vince when he returned from one of his shopping trips and warned him that if he caught him leaving site without telling him again, or if he bought any more stolen goods to site, he would have to involve me and inevitably the police. Vince was a very stupid man and told Curly to mind his own business in very colourful language. There were only two hits, one when Curly hit him and the second when Vince hit the floor. I got the whole story from my spy, the canteen manager, who of course overheard everything in the canteen and couldn't wait to fill me in on the details. I got Vince's version of the story which was slightly different from the truth and sacked him on the spot. This was before employment tribunal's, and I could manage without Vince but not without Curly; job done.

As the project came to an end, and in the normal rush to meet the contract completion date with the floor coverings having just been completed from being laid, there seemed to be rather a lot of carpet left over. I didn't question this as it certainly wasn't unusual to have materials left at the end of such a large project.

At this time Jen and I wanted to move to a larger individual property on a bigger piece of land so had the spare carpet delivered home in anticipation of this. About a week later my carpenter foreman, Geoff Tomsett, came to me in a bit of a sweat saying that he had been checking a large room off for completion when he had discovered that the floor covering that had been laid was vinyl when it should have been carpet. I decided to let sleeping dogs lie and wait to see what happened. Nobody ever mentioned it and the carpet came in very handy in our new home.

The Bristow project was completed, and I was kicking my heels waiting to be posted to my next place of work, so Jen and I decided to spend some time looking for our next house. We didn't only want a larger house we wanted one that was older with potential that we could extend and refurbish. We had been on the lookout for about 18 months and had found exactly what we wanted in a property named 'Leacroft' in a village called Bolney – not very far away from where we were living. It was detached, sat on about a third of an acre of land, and needed a lot of work done to upgrade it. Unfortunately for us it was another house we couldn't afford but had fallen in love with and that we desperately wanted. We made an offer which was rejected and the property was sold to another couple, we were very disappointed to say the least. When we were looking again at the end of Bristow's we went back to Bolney to see if there were any properties similar to the one we had seen before. To our complete surprise and delight 'our house' was up for sale again. We immediately called the agents and arranged a viewing. It turned out that the couple that had purchased the house had split up after they had a baby and were in the process of getting divorced and both wanted their money out as quickly as possible. Not knowing how I was going to raise the money, I vowed to Jen that nothing would stop us getting 'our house' this time. We offered the asking price, not wanting to haggle in case we lost out again. We put our house up for sale in Hurstpierpoint straight away, but several weeks passed without a sale or indeed much interest in it. The owners of the Bolney house gave us an ultimatum, set the wheels in motion with a definite completion date immediately or they were going to put the house back on the market. We had arranged the additional mortgage to cover the difference between the sale of Hurstpierpoint and the purchase of Bolney but couldn't proceed until we had sold our house. I was at a complete loss at what to do, Jen had set her heart on the new property and I had said we would have it. I was sitting in my office on site thinking and trying to come up with an idea of how to raise the money we needed and thought of contacting my boss, Ray Perkins, to see if he had any bright ideas. I made the phone call at the end of the day, but it was picked up by Peter Longley, our company chairman, who shared an office with Ray. "Hello, Peter Longley here", he said. I apologised for disturbing him and said that I was trying to contact Ray. "I'm sorry" came the reply, "but Ray is out for the rest of the day, can I help?". "No, its OK" I said, "I'll contact him another time". Peter Longley went on to explain that Ray was away for a long weekend and wouldn't be back until the following week, my heart sank. The chairman must have detected something in my voice, "are you sure I can't help?" he said, sounding rather insistent. With that I took a deep breath and our future into my hands and outlined what my problem was. He didn't interrupt me and said nothing until I had explained everything, when he simply said "I'm going to be in my office until quite late why don't you drop in on your way home and we could have a talk, I'll wait until you arrive". It was about 7 o'clock when I arrived at Peter Longley's office door, not knowing what ideas he was going to come up with but I was rather hoping that he may at least point me in a direction where I may be able to get a bank bridging loan without much security. I knocked on his door and heard a voice shout for me to go in. I was welcomed in and asked to sit down and run through what I had already been over on the phone but to also explain and set out my financial position and how much money it would take to buy the house, which I did. I went on to explain that 'Leacroft' was for sale for £24,000. It doesn't sound much now but it was a huge amount of money at the time, you could still buy a reasonable house for half that amount. Our chairman listened patiently and when I came to the end of my explanation he reached down into his desk drawer, got out a cheque book, and wrote and signed a cheque in my favour for the full price of the house. "There you are" he just said, "go and buy your house". I sat there with my mouth wide open, I was speechless, what could I say to someone who had just handed over such a vast sum of money. I asked when the money had to be paid back by, to which the reply was "when you have completed the whole transaction". I then asked what the interest on the loan would be, to which he replied that we would talk about that when everything was completed. I went on to ask what guarantee he would require that the money would be paid back, his reply was heart tearing "why, are you going somewhere then?". In the end we sold our house in Hurstpierpoint and when the mortgage was all in place and everything had been sorted 6 months later I made arrangements to meet Peter Longley to repay the debt. Again, I brought up the thorny point of interest that I owed to which the answer was "no there won't be any interest Richard". What an amazing man our chairman was. I have never met anyone apart from his father, Sir Norman Longley, who would have done such a thing for me, and I might add that he was just very shrewd in his own way. It took me a long time to work it out. He had hitched me to the firm for the rest of my working life and had obtained my loyalty. I am so proud to be able to say I never ever let him or the firm down, I would have done anything for him after that. I was still only 31-years-old.

Chapter 10
Still Climbing

Sutton Civic Offices in 1976 was the next on my list of projects and was by far the largest, and had the biggest budget. It was on this contract that I was to come in contact with the person who was to become one of the biggest influences on my career and indeed my whole future, his name was John Ebdon. John was a director of the firm and only about 4 years older than me and my hardest taskmaster. He was without any doubt the most ambitious person I have ever met, he was also to become a great friend to me and my family. He already had quite a reputation and not all of it good, behind his back he was referred to as 'God' and I could understand why, he was going to the top and nobody was going to stop him. I just decided to go with him. I could see that my new boss lacked some of the things that I had, which were extensive site experience and a tradesman's knowledge together with a background of hard knocks from my working-class background. What I lacked, John had in bundles and vice versa. I was going to have to learn a lot from him and fast. John had an assistant by the name of Colin Guest who was to be the contract manager for the project. Colin was a very nice person, very religious, with a string of academic qualifications to his name but lacked my site experience. I got on very well with Colin and liked him very much except he was a bit too laid back for my liking. My impatience wanted everything done immediately, or sooner.

I took Curly and all his men, along with Geoff my carpenter foreman, with me which helped to get the project underway in the shortest possible time. I then had one of the greatest strokes of luck in all my time in the industry, and he arrived just after we had got the job up and running. John had told me that he was going to send me an assistant who, when I first laid eyes on him, I thought was someone looking for a job as a labourer and not a very smart one at that. He had long hair down to his shoulders, looked as if he needed a good scrub and introduced himself as Peter Weeks. Another lesson learnt: 'never judge a book by its cover'. Peter was sharp, conscientious, easy for me to get on with, disagreed with me if he thought I was wrong and worked his socks off. We became friends and colleagues for over 30 years. Peter and I with our team pushed and pushed to get as far ahead of the programme as possible. It was at this point that the penny dropped with me as to why I always found it difficult to get along with the architects I had worked with. Most, if not all of them, didn't want to, shall we say, overwork themselves and found it difficult when they were put under pressure to produce information quickly to keep up with progress on site. As I always issued information requirement dates at the start of each project and then monitored it throughout, it always showed them up in a bad light if progress slowed. During the construction process we had many ups and downs as it was the time when our Prime Minister, Mrs Thatcher, decided to pick a fight with the coal mining industry. We had delays due to power blackouts and what were known as 'flying pickets', coal miners from all over the country stopping workers and materials entering our site. Peter had a hobby which came in useful from time to time which was weightlifting and had muscles that I didn't know existed. He was a very big boy even at only 22-years-old. We were desperate for a delivery of materials, many of which were becoming in short supply, when a delivery turned up on site.

All this made life a bit more difficult for me as I had a lot of sympathy with the cause of the miners. I had been a union member myself and could so easily have been drawn further into the movement.

At this point a delivery of steel reinforcement turned up at the site entrance which the pickets had descended on earlier in the day. The usual threats and banter went on when one of the pickets asked the driver of the lorry what would happen if one of the pickets laid down behind the rear wheels of the truck, to which the driver replied "He will get f*****g squashed". All hell broke loose. The pickets were trying to get the driver out of his cab, punches were being thrown between the miners and the driver's mate. I could see what was happening from my office window, so I grabbed Peter and out we went. I let him lead on this occasion, where he quickly restored order. Peter opened the site gate and in rolled the delivery lorry. It was quickly unloaded, the crisis was over and more importantly I was in one piece and the job could progress.

On another occasion we had a rather aggressive bricklayer on site who had been to the local pub during the lunch period and had come back on to site without my knowledge. I was alerted to the problem by the bricklayer foreman who said that the man was threatening to stove my head in. I can't remember why, but I sent him straight away to find Peter. In the meantime, the bricklayer came storming into my office brandishing his trowel. Before I could find anywhere less obvious, I backed myself away from him, but he had me in the corner behind my desk. Then, to my relief, in burst Peter followed by Curly. One swift move and they were on him and I showed my bravery by sacking him on the spot; another job done.

The union organiser for the area we were in was a very aggressive person and based in London where he seemed to have a lot of control over the national contractors' labour. As it happened I got on with the man very well but not until I had explained to him that I had been a tradesman, union member and fully understood his position. We would always chat over the problems of the time, putting the world to right over a cup of tea and a cheese roll, but I always made sure that Peter and Curly were not far away!

Rates of pay for our employees were always a point of contention as it was governed by the rates set down between the employers and the unions which sometimes favoured sub-contractors over our own men. We, as a company, operated a bonus system based on the amount of production for each trade and this was the area over which I had most discretion. I made sure that my men were always at the top end when it came to pay. I knew how hard they all worked, and if I thought they deserved it they received the maximum I thought I could get away with, irrespective of what the official calculations were. This was the main way I found to motivate my workforce but there were other ways which cost very little. One method was to organise a football match every Christmas between the men and the managers – Peter and Curly were always on my side. The build-up to the match would start weeks before with threats of all sorts being made to disable my side. They never did as I was the referee and played at the same time. Kick off was late morning and then following the match the site was abandoned for the rest of the day when we all went to the pub. Curly was always in charge of finances where he had several ways of raising money throughout the rest of the year, two of which were the sale of any spare reinforcement and, the other, charges made to sub-contractors for any special favours or assistance.

In the end the Sutton Offices project turned out very well in spite of the miners' problems. It was completed 6 months early and made a stomping profit of over half a million pounds more than any other in the company's history. It has stuck in my mind ever since as I was given the sum of £1,000 as a bonus and that was even taxed, I was not impressed.

Time again moved on and my team and I were moved on to other contracts, all of which were finished on time and made a profit. Due to the size of the projects increasing, another manager joined our team. Two or 3 months passed, and I received a phone call from the local police to say they had this new manager in custody and that he had given my name and telephone number for a reference. I was shocked but confirmed who the man was along with his address etc. and waited to see what happened next. After a couple of hours, our man turned up. I got him in the office, sat him down, and asked him to explain. He said he had gone into a supermarket, picked up a number of items before discovering that he didn't have any money with him, so he decided to try to get out without paying and got caught. I didn't believe a word of what he said but I could also see that whatever had happened had been a big mistake on his part. He begged me not to dismiss him or tell the firm, and that his marriage was in serious difficulties and this would finish it and him. I sent him outside and told him to carry on as if nothing had happened and to come back and see me at the end of the day when everyone had left the site. After all the personnel had left at the end of the day, in he came to the office. I could see from his face that he was so worried. I had already made up my mind to give him a second chance, but I didn't tell him until he had been given the thick end of my tongue and warned that if I heard even a whisper of any further problems he would be gone in a flash. No mention was to be made to anyone else and I promised to keep his secret which, with the exception of Jen, I have kept to this very day. It never hurts to have someone owe you a favour.

After plenty of thought on my part I decided it was time for me to move on from site management, so the next time John Ebdon visited site I asked him for a meeting to discuss my future. When we sat down together later that day I explained that I felt it was time for me to move onto the next stage on the career ladder, contract management. I went on to say that I had nothing further to prove, either to myself or the company, and pointed out that none of the contracts that I had ever built with my team had ever been late finishing and had all made a profit. John listened to what I had to say and promised to take what I had said on board and to come back to me. As a major regional contractor, I fully understood that appointing or promoting staff could not happen overnight. If we had been one of the bigger national ones then it was much easier to have spare capacity, but we could not afford that. I also knew that I had a rival in the firm who was also wanting to get promoted and he came under John's sphere of control. He had always been ahead of me in the pecking order, so I knew this could pose a problem for John. A few weeks later I was summoned to head office. After a short discussion I was handed a set of architects' and engineers' drawings and all the contract documents for the construction of the first phase of the redevelopment of Goodwood racecourse. I had got my way and I was to be promoted to resident contract manager with a considerable uplift in salary and a new car to fit my new position. I took all the drawings and paperwork home with me and spent the next few days studying them and getting familiar with the needs of the project.

As the company grew and expanded over future years, specialist staff were recruited who produced programmes, progress reports, ordered materials, appointed subcontractors and many other functions. None of this was available when I set out in contract management, you had to do it all yourself and that suited me just fine.

It didn't take long for me to realise that the design and construction process for the grandstand was completely new to me, all the structure was to be made off site in precast reinforced concrete and assembled on site like a giant jigsaw puzzle. The architects were The Lobb Partnership led by the senior partner Jim Cutlack, a very experienced person and one of the only architects that I truly respected. Jim had a wonderful way about him which included a sense of humour (architects generally don't have a sense of humour). We hit it off from the beginning and went on to work together for many years on several different projects. We never disagreed on anything and always found a way forward on any problems that arose, his wife however was a different matter!

Our engineers were Jan Bobrowski and Partners, led by Jan himself with his brother Alex – both of whom were refugees from Poland and had walked across Europe to escape the

Germans in WW2. Jan was a pure genius in the design of precast concrete, he once said that his aim was to be able to design concrete that could be rolled up in lengths. I'm still waiting. At the outset he sat down with me to explain his design in detail and how he intended the structure should be assembled. Each section of concrete was to be made in Norfolk by a company named Anglian Building Products and transported to Goodwood to be assembled. My first task was to draw up a detailed day-by-day, hour-by-hour delivery schedule and issue it to the manufacturer to ensure each section was made in the right order to meet my programme. Getting the structure made and assembled on site as quickly as possible was the key to the whole project, not least because the overall construction period was only 39 weeks. The main festival race meeting was to take place on July 29th 1979 without fail, no pressure then.

As I had moved up the management ladder so had my right-hand man Peter Weeks, and he was now the senior site manager. Fortunately, I had an office in a separate building away from the site offices where I could do my job and allow Peter to get on with his without any interference from me. Each section of the frame arrived in the correct order by road with the exception of the main 30 tonne spine beams which were delivered to Chichester station and then transferred to the site by road. On completion of the main concrete frame and the fixing of the main support cables, we got straight on with the fitting out work. All was on programme at the beginning of October 1978.

During the progress of the contract a young architect was assigned to the project, based on site to resolve design problems quickly, and his name was Mark (I've forgotten his surname). He was a heavy smoker, I was not and I was the only member of my family apart from Mum that didn't smoke. I continually nagged Mark in an attempt to stop what I thought was his disgusting habit. To prove how bad it was for his health (and mine) I challenged him to a running race to show him how fit he could be, just like me. The challenge was arranged to follow a site progress meeting, when all the team would be there to see me humiliate Mark and shame him into stopping smoking. The prize for the winner was £10 paid by the loser. I was very confident and told him so. As soon as the race started it was over, when Mark took off like a rocket leaving me standing. I was well beaten. What he or anyone else had failed to tell me was that Mark had been his county's sprint champion and still ran; what I failed to tell him was that I was so unfit.

The weather that winter could not have been worse. Snow and ice we could have managed but, no, it had to be one of the wettest for years on top of the South Downs. Every day we could see the dark clouds sweeping in from the Isle of Wight to the southwest of us. It came in horizontally day after day. We struggled on until Christmas. Peter and his team were doing all they could to make progress but still falling behind programme. After Christmas the weather was not much improved and by Easter 1979 the end seemed further away. Unbeknown to me, the site had a visitor late on a very wet afternoon. Our chairman Peter Longley decided to turn up unannounced after reading my latest progress report. The result of this was that he returned to Crawley head office to announce his findings and opinion, which of course he had every right to do. He was of the view that the project would not be finished on time and that the architects, and therefore the client, should be advised of that. He also said that all temporary steps should be put in place so that some of the building could be used, for example temporary toilets.

Just before Easter we were still struggling, mainly because the contractor who had been specified to manufacture the roof lights had not met their designated fixing date thus preventing the building being made watertight. I had tried and tried to get the contractor's senior management to site to sort out the problem without success. So, with our prompting, Jim Cutlack called an emergency meeting on site on Easter Sunday and demanded that the roof light contractor and the whole team should attend. Myself and John Ebdon, as our director, attended along with everyone else including Mr Stuart Rutter the sub-contractor's man who I had been trying to get to site for weeks. Once the meeting got underway Rutter was full of excuses, none of which held up under close questioning helped by the detailed records I had kept of all past events including phone calls and the dates and times. Mr Rutter was full of apologies and promises. I didn't believe any of it and said so, but everyone except John and I were willing to give him one last chance.

After the meeting, Lord March invited us back to Goodwood House for drinks in the library, so John and I locked up the site and made our way down to the house to join the party. When we walked in I couldn't believe my eyes, there was Rutter – the reason we had all had to give up our Easter Sunday – with Lord March and his father, the Duke of Richmond, being given the royal treatment as if he was the contract saviour. I turned to John and said, "If this is what you get for creating havoc and failure then you and I are in line for a knighthood out of this job". I'm still waiting. This story has been told so many time over the years. We both found it so ironic that the one person who had failed got the most attention. Mr Rutter was even invited to the opening celebrations when the contract was completed, but we didn't forget when it came to settle his final account – every dog has his day!

Against all the odds, Peter and his team managed to complete everything on time and make a healthy profit. As far as I was concerned that was all that mattered as it could have been curtains for my career into higher management.

Just before the end it was announced that Her Majesty the Queen was to carry out the official opening of the project. John called at our house one Friday evening to discuss the arrangements and agree who should represent the firm. I was sitting talking about this when I suddenly felt very dizzy with the most violent pain in my side and back and passed out. Jen and John both thought I was having a heart attack, which it could have been with the enormous pressure that I had been under over the previous months. The emergency services were called,

*The leadership team for the Goodwood Race Course.
Centre: Lord March (later the Duke of Richmond); Jim Cutlack (second from left); John Ebdon (fourth from right) with
members of the Horse Racing Levy Board. Mark Talbot,
winner of our running race, on the far right.*

and I was soon rushed away to the hospital where it was found after tests that I
was suffering from stones in my kidneys –
one of which had decided to find its way
through my system and got stuck. I have
suffered from this problem on several occasions since and can honestly say it is a
pain to be avoided and not something to
be recommended.

It was decided that John, Peter and I
were to be presented to Her Majesty and
soon the great day arrived when each of
us was spoken to individually. When it
came to my turn her Majesty said how
lucky she thought we were that the win-
ter had been so mild. I couldn't stop myself explaining to our monarch and head of state to
so many countries around the world that it may have been mild but it had rained almost
non-stop on our grandstand, and considerably held up progress. She smiled at me and moved
on. Throughout my working life I have disagreed about many things with a great number of
people but this one must take the biscuit.

With my first contract under my belt in my new position I was given several projects to run
within my own group, each supervised by a site management team. I moved into head office
with an assistant and a small team of surveyors. At first, I had shared a secretary with John but
now I was on the lookout for my own so decided to take on a temporary one from an agency. I
had one or two turn up but not people I thought I would be able to get along with long-term,
until one morning a French lady appeared and told me she was my new temporary secretary.
Her name was Marie José Gazeres de Baradieu. I thought that this arrangement would last
about an hour, but I got that wrong as we stayed together for the next 18 years until I retired.
Marie José was not only my secretary, she was, and is, a good friend who defended me from
anyone who dared to say a word about me with which she disagreed. Both her and her partner,
Richard (her second after me, as I have always told her) are still our friends 38 years on, not
bad for a temp.

On the back of the success at Goodwood we were invited to a meeting with the directors
of Cheltenham Racecourse to discuss the first phase of the complete redevelopment of the
grandstands and the facilities there. Many weeks later, following selection and negotiations,
we secured the first contract. We were fortunate that the archchitects, engineers and quantity
surveyors were the same as Goodwood so we had nothing to prove except that it was off

The completed grandstand at Cheltenham Racecourse, early 1980s.

our normal patch. Having a project a long way away from our base in the southwest of the country was something new to me and so needed a lot of thought of how to staff it. My thoughts went towards our tried and trusted team of Peter & co., but convincing them to live away from home for a year was something I had to do. I needed people I could trust. After some negotiations on working hours, pay and a living allowance they were convinced to go and were augmented by other members of staff from my group, again all people I had faith in, knew and would not let me down. It was also agreed that the company would buy a house in the area, furnish it and hire a housekeeper to look after everyone. All I had to do was find the house and someone to look after the troops. The house we needed had to be reasonably close to the racecourse and be large enough to accommodate all our people, with at least four double bedrooms with single beds and a large kitchen dining room.

I trawled all the local estate agents and viewed many properties, but none met with my criteria. Just as I was about to give up and come up with alternative ideas, I was introduced to an elderly couple by a different estate agent. When I met them they told me that their house had been on the market for over a year, and they were keen to sell and move as quickly as possible. I walked around the house and saw immediately it was perfect for what we wanted. It was in good order, reasonably well decorated and above all spotless. I hadn't been in the house more than 5 minutes when I told the couple that we would buy it subject to the company's approval of the price which I would recommend. I shall never forget the look on the faces of the elderly couple, they couldn't believe their luck. It had all taken 20 minutes from my arrival at their front door.

As the years went by my management team carried out further phases of the development at Cheltenham as well as at Goodwood (for some reason Lobb Partnership were not retained by Goodwood and I never did find out why). We also went on to build a new grandstand at Fontwell Park and Kempton Park, other supermarkets for Sainsbury's, Tesco and Waitrose, a new town centre called Piries Place at Horsham, several office blocks in Crawley, schools in various locations and so many projects it's difficult to record and mention them all. Suffice to say I was kept very busy with my hair changing from bright red to grey in a fairly short space of time.

It was during one of the projects at Cheltenham that my old friend Bill Tustin, from a company called Littlehampton Welding Limited, produced at a site meeting one of his classic moves to get himself off the hook for being behind programme. Everyone was sitting around the table when in walked Bill to give his report to the team. As the chairman, I asked for a copy of his report, which he didn't present but instead slapped a heavy hammer on the table with a handful of nails and said to me, "I know you're going to crucify me, so I thought I would bring the tools for you to do it with". We all collapsed laughing and Bill was off the hook, all he needed was some time until the next progress report when he was back on programme. I knew Bill for years and put a great deal of work with his company, giving him many chances to work with us even when he was not the most competitive (cheapest). We still exchange Christmas cards and I hear from time to time how he is, but he did cross me once when he suggested to me that I was trying to get something for nothing from him for myself. I wasn't and never would from anyone – I never forget Bill.

During the construction works at Cheltenham, I was invited to lunch following each site meeting by the directors of the course. It was at one of these occasions that I witnessed one of the most awful racial comments. I was sat next to a man, by a name I won't reveal, who was a member of the royal staff. The story went like this: As the Queen Mother always came to the Cheltenham Gold Cup meeting the question was asked if she would be attending that year. This person responded (in the most exaggerated plummy voice) that "Her Majesty is absolutely furious with the Foreign Office because she is unable to attend this year". The cry went up, "Oh, why?". He went on, "The Foreign Office has arranged for a head of state to visit on the very day, we wouldn't mind but he's a bloody black man". I sat there shocked, not only by what he had said but by the fact that nobody took him to task, from which I could only think that they all must have agreed with him. It never ceased to surprise me that most people that I dealt with in senior positions, and especially the wealthy clients or so called upper classes, assumed that my politics were the same as theirs, i.e. Conservative and right wing, little did they know. I have always kept my feet well and truly on the ground and I attempt to never forget my roots and who I am.

I attended numerous opening ceremonies attended by politicians, local dignitaries, people who thought they were important and some that knew they weren't. It's funny how so many were interested when all the hard work had been done. We had one more visit from the Queen at Epsom College, and it was nice to see her for a second time. I was also presented to Her Majesty, the Queen Mother, when we completed the new facilities at Kempton Park racecourse. When she went to shake my hand I couldn't help but notice her dirty and broken finger nails. It was said she liked gardening, but I never imagined she did it herself. She invited a few people, including me, into the new Royal Box, chatting away and reminding me of my Nan Constable. However, I don't think she had to take her sheets and the King's best and only suit to the pawnbrokers on Monday mornings.

Throughout my working life I have always tried to keep my feet well and truly on the ground and never forgetting where I had come from and where my roots are. Mixing with so many people from all walks of life can sometimes make this very difficult and I did let my guard down on one occasion.

I had been invited to a private dinner party at the Dorchester Hotel Park Lane, in London, one of the most prestigious hotels in the world. It was to be an evening dress occasion to be held in a private dining room for about twelve guests. I arrived at the hotel in plenty of time by taxi where the doorman opened the door for me to exit in style, I was very impressed. I think it was at this moment that I started to get a bit carried away and thinking that I had arrived at my rightful place in the world. All went well at the dinner and I had had a thoroughly enjoyable evening meeting and chatting with the other guests before it was time to go. I was presented with my overcoat by one of the staff, said my goodbyes to the other guests and my thanks to our host; this was the life for me, far away from those cold dirty old building sites.

I swept down to the main entrance of the hotel thinking I would just get the doorman to call me a taxi without delay. I saw the man in the bright red coat and top hat standing outside and indicated for him to call me the taxi. His reply was sharp and to the point, "Certainly sir, would you like to stand in the queue with everyone else". I looked to my right where about a dozen people were waiting and I'm sure they all had a grin on their faces.

I had been put firmly in my place, I really should have known better. As my mum would have said, "That's for trying to get above your station" – and she would have been right. I never fell into that trap again.

Life in the construction business has always been either overrun with work or twiddling your thumbs and wondering where the next contract would come from, and we like others went through some very lean times. I never liked working for developers, in my view no builder worth his salt should go anywhere near them – they are unscrupulous, unreasonable, thuggish, full of greed and should be avoided like the plague. In bad times we could not be picky and had to take what we could get but my goodness how I hated ninety-nine percent of them.

One such client developer, and there were many of a similar type, was from eastern Europe and we managed to get ourselves contracted to build a nightclub and leisure centre for them in East Grinstead. It soon became apparent that the design team were terrified of the client and as far as we were concerned a complete dead loss. I had been told by the site manager that at one site meeting the boss of the outfit turned up with what he could only describe as bodyguards and was convinced that they were carrying guns inside their jacket pockets. I took some convincing on this but on reflection afterwards I'm not so sure. We fought our way through to the completion of the contract and were trying to settle the final account to be paid and in my eyes to get as far away from them as possible. John and I were summoned to a meeting in the nightclub and when we arrived we were ushered down into the basement. In the centre of the dance floor was a long table with two spotlights shining down on it and surrounded by chairs with a number of people sitting down waiting, it would seem, for us to arrive. All other lighting had been turned down low. The design team were there, all of whom had obviously been giving the story of the project and how they wanted it to be seen by the boss of the business who sat at the end of the table. John and I were told to take our place at the opposite end. After a short interlude, the discussions got underway on the final settlement of our account, having been briefed by my senior surveyor. The design team started to disagree with everything I said. Our site manager, Jerry Hanson, was a very methodical person and had kept very good records throughout the contract so I was able to set about demolishing the replies and pointing out the shortcomings of what I considered the opposition. I was looking towards the boss when he suddenly jumped up in the air and started to scream and shout in a language not known to me, or anyone else I suspect. He picked up the chair he was sitting on and threw it across the room into the darkness, then grabbed the end of the table and tossed it into the air still screaming with rage. More chairs and anything else he could lay his hands on also followed. I grabbed my papers and briefcase, got hold of John's jacket sleeve, and made for the exit stairs and didn't stop until we reached our car. In the end we were able to get paid most of our money but not without a struggle and threats of court action.

We were told a cheque was ready for our collection at an address just outside the town. John and I were detailed to go and collect it. Off we went full of trepidation to find the address of a farm we were told to go to. Behind the entrance gates were two barking Alsatian dogs running loose and displaying rather large teeth. John was driving. "Jump out and open the gates", he said. Now everyone who knows me is aware that I have a dislike for dogs, big ones in particular, along with any other form of pet. There was no way that I was even getting out of the car let alone opening any gate and told John that if he wanted the gate open he would have to do it himself. Out of the car he got and opened the gate, the dogs stopped barking and he started stroking them. I made sure the window of the car was closed and the door safely locked. We drove up the track pursued by John's new canine friends expecting to be met by some more undesirables but, after looking all around (John, not me), we decided the place had been abandoned or at least been locked up for some time. It didn't take much to convince us to leave and to try to get our money in a safer environment. We did eventually get paid but I didn't like the experience one bit.

≈ * ≈

Chapter 11
Emma and Mathew

As the years passed, Emma and Mathew were growing up and heading towards their teenage years. If I am honest I missed quite a lot of what went on due to my own fault in being so immersed in my work. It's not until now that I have realised this when they talk about things that I had no idea went on. I did make sure that I attended all the school plays, functions and end of term ballet classes with Emma, on many occasions I was the only father in attendance. I did spend a lot of time watching Mathew play football from the age of 9 until he finished playing in his mid-20s. I'm not sure who enjoyed it more – him or me. I even had the indignity of being sent off in one match when he was playing centre forward for Cuckfield Cosmos. All through the first half he was being kicked all over the place by one of the opposition, with the referee doing nothing about it. In the second half of the game I just exploded at the ref. His action took me by surprise when he stopped the game and called me over to him. I was in no mood to move and explained to him that if he wanted to talk to me HE could come on over to me. The referee took out his red card and showed it to me by waving it in the air and officially sending me off of the field of play. As I wasn't on it, I stopped where I was, and he just blew the whistle and the game carried on. Mathew and the rest of the family thought this episode very funny and still remind me, 35 plus years later, of when Dad got sent off at football when he wasn't even playing.

I was sitting in the garden one hot summer's day after spending several hours cutting grass when out of the blue I started to think how nice it would be to have our own swimming pool. After discussions between us all it was decided to go ahead and build it ourselves, which we did along the side of the house. Jen, Emma and Mathew all joined in with mixing cement, laying the concrete blocks and all the hard work in making a dream come true – it was a real joint effort.

In 1991 it was time to enclose the pool and as usual we decided to do some of the work ourselves with a steel frame supplied by my old friends at Littlehampton Welding Ltd. I was to supply and fix the sliding glazed doors and the roof glazing, with a subcontractor building the brickwork. All went to plan until New Year's Eve when I started fixing the roof glazing.

Emma and Mathew in the 1970s.

When lunch time came around, Jen called me to come down off the roof. As I stepped on the ladder it gave way. Down I went and in trying to save myself I shot out my right arm and got it caught between the ladder rung and a horizontal scaffold pole, crushing my elbow. I managed to get my arm free and get into the house, telling Jen what had happened on the way. When I got to the hall I passed out and collapsed on the floor underneath the Christmas tree. Mathew called the emergency services and I was carted away in the ambulance. Once at the hospital it took a while to be seen and have X-rays taken and then we were told that nobody was available until the following Monday to do anything. I was in a lot of pain and Jen was adamant that something had to be done, but only a skeleton staff was available. After mentioning that we had private healthcare insurance everything swung into action and I was in the operating theatre by 4 o'clock, having an operation carried out by the senior orthopaedic surgeon complete with all his team – money always talks. The damage to my arm was extensive, leaving me with about 20% less feeling in my right hand and my elbow in a fixed position so that I am unable to straighten my right arm. I only had myself to blame and should have known better as I had spent years telling other people to make sure all ladders were tied in position to prevent accidents.

Boys started to appear on the scene with Emma and I found this very difficult to deal with. We had always been very close and I was now expected to stand aside, not something I have been very good at. A boy arrived at our house one day who I took an instant dislike to, for no other reason (honest) except that I have a sixth sense gathered over many years with dealing with all sorts of people. I'm not willing to go into any further details except to say he had to go and I made sure he did. Nobody has ever actually told me, but my understanding is that my intuition was later proved right. I rest my case.

Mathew on the other hand kept everything, as far as girlfriends were concerned, close to his chest. To us he seemed to change his girls almost as often as his underclothes. I just knew I didn't like any of them much until I met my lovely daughter-in law, Sam, thank God.

Soon after Mathew had passed his driving test we went on holiday and left him Jen's car to drive while we were away. All was fine until we arrived back home and found that Mathew had been involved in an accident. His story went something like this: "I was driving gently along the country lane when a fox ran out in front of the car. I took avoiding action and finished up going through a hedge, turning the car onto its side". I was not convinced. He continued,

"There was a bull in the field and I had to sit on top of the car for ages before it was distracted, and I was able to make my escape". I was even less convinced. We were so thankful that he wasn't injured in any way that we let it drop and said no more, especially as Emma had already sorted out the repairs etc., and we didn't want to make things any worse than they already were. My son may be able to stretch the truth to others, and he may think he has convinced me of other things over the years, but he hasn't. I always know when, but he doesn't know how I know. I shall keep my secret!

I am not prepared to admit to many mistakes in my life but there is one that I am willing to put into print for the record, it involved Emma. Based on her academic qualifications, for history, she was selected for interview at Oxford University. I took her to the interview but in the mean time I, in all my wisdom, questioned what job she thought she would get with a history degree – so she had decided to study law. Oh, my ignorance and stupidity, which I can only put down to my living through the 1940s and 50s when the only thought was to get a job, any job! Emma's version of this is that she applied to read History at Oxford but they didn't like the fact she had applied to do Law at other universities. Plus, outside of Oxford and Cambridge, Leeds was the best place to read Law, with a fabulous reputation, so it all worked out. Why I thought I knew all the answers, who knows? Emma didn't get accepted and I have blamed myself ever since. I tell myself that you can only do what you think is right when bringing up your children, but it is little consolation. This one I got very wrong. Emma also went on to say that it was the Oxford College she applied to that was wrong, as it was predominantly private school boys and the head boy of Eton was there when she was being interviewed.

In the end Emma went to Leeds University and did a law degree and when the day came for us to leave we were all feeling very sad and worried. So, on the way up to Leeds I put a Stevie Wonder song on to cheer us up: 'I Just Called to Say I Love You'. It only made things worse. I have never been able to listen to this song without feeling sad. From that day to this, it still brings a lump to my throat. After leaving Emma to settle in, Jen and I drove all the way home in silence. When we arrived home I went to our bedroom and broke down and cried. Bringing up your children is not easy.

Three years soon passed and before we knew it we were attending her graduation and she was on her way to Chester to attend law school, where she passed her exams in the top grade to allow her to qualify as a solicitor. She seemed to be surprised that she did so well, we weren't. We attended the presentation ceremony at the Law Society Hall and for passing we celebrated with tea at the Savoy.

Mathew had a different approach to study and university in that everything was always left until the last minute, including any studying. Like Emma he couldn't make up his mind what he was going to do. As he had been working on some of my building sites from when he was quite young I stuck my two-penny worth in and encouraged him to study quantity surveying. My reasoning was that it was much less stressful than being at the sharp end of the construction business and I would be able to help him. Why he chose to do his degree in Kingston-upon-Thames I still have no idea to this day, it was a total failure. Without going into details, Mathew dropped out. I was at my wits end to know what to do for the best. As he had started a course the rules were that to do another we had to meet the full cost. I started to wonder if it was worth it and gave him a job labouring on site until the problem could be resolved. He didn't let me down and worked like a dog and earned some money at the same time. After a lot of heartache, we decided between us that if I could get him in he would embark on a Construction Management degree at Brighton University which would enable him to live at home. I managed to buy him one of the firm's old vans and had it sprayed blue so that it wasn't too obvious where it's past life had been. This didn't stop him from being pulled over by the police at all hours of the night, but it did get him around.

My biggest concern was that Mathew would lose interest in the course and stray again, once bitten twice shy. I loved him too much to let him fall down a hole again and was absolutely determined that he was not going to finish up going through what I had years before. I had been driven for years by the thought of my two children not having a proper education. For me there has never been a question of going back, it simply was not an option I was willing to accept.

I had one last trick up my sleeve to ensure Mathew kept on the right track. At the firm we had a very close relationship with Brighton University, in that we always tried to recruit the top graduating building students from them. I also knew the principal of the construction department, Mr Rutter, and managed to enrol Mathew for the next academic year with a further agreement that I would have a verbal update from Mr Rutter on a regular basis without Mathew's knowledge. All turned out well and we were able to attend his graduation with enormous pride that he had battled through. I must point out that since that first set-back, Mathew worked very hard and joined me at the firm when he had completed his studies. I consider him to be a better administrator than I ever was and he became a director of a construction company at a much earlier age than I was able to. What more could I ask?

≈ * ≈

Chapter 12
Reaching my Goal and Beyond

It was a glorious day in 1986 when John Ebdon gave me some very good news. I was in his office and just about to leave when he said he had something to tell me in strictest confidence. I was all ears and wondering what was coming next, you always had to be on your toes with John as he didn't suffer fools gladly. He went on to tell me that at a board meeting held earlier in the day it had been decided to offer me a directorship of the company. If I'm honest about it, I was not surprised. Nobody had worked harder for it than me, but I was aware that my closest rivals may not be so happy. I was very proud to have made it to board level and couldn't get it out of my head how my Dad had started the ball rolling all those years before. I felt he had been justified in giving me my chance against his better judgement, something he had denied my brothers. He would have been so proud of me.

I was given a new role of 'contracts director', responsible for all work carried out by the company's head office which accounted for the greater part of the turnover and the most profitable. Other branch offices were run by different directors and I had the added responsibility of our plant department and the overseeing of about 150 company cars, vans, people carriers and lorries, all of the company plant requirements and the electrical department who installed the temporary electrics on all the company sites.

Everything went fine and much the same with the added responsibilities for the next 6 or 7 years before the industry was hit by another drastic downturn in workload. We fought our way on, but things got worse and worse when it was decided to shut the branch offices in London, Basingstoke and Faversham. The directors at the first two were made redundant and Faversham was sold off. All outstanding contracts, and their problems, of which there were many, were transferred to me. We were pushed into a position where I had to make ninety-five percent of our directly employed tradesmen redundant, a lot of them with many years' service to the company, and I had the job of telling them – I hated it.

John had been made joint managing director when I had joined the board, but all the problems got to him and I was concerned for his health and told him so. It wasn't long before he retired on health grounds, and I was on my own – or at least that's how it felt to me. We struggled on for a few years when the Longley family decided to sell the company, which in

On the occasion of my 25th anniversary with James Longley & Co., and receiving a handshake from the Chairman, Oliver Longley (circa 1984).

time they did. Before that, we had obtained a large contract against my better judgement for Dell (the computer company), but our client was a developer. I could see it was going to be a recipe for disaster as we had taken on the design and construction of the project, both things in my view we should have never touched.

I put my old senior manager Peter Weeks in charge. At least I had someone I could trust on site. Peter, I have said before, was a scruffy so-and-so and didn't come up to the suave sophistication expected by the client, but that had never been a problem before in all the years we had worked together. The client's representative took an instant dislike to Peter and insisted I met him on site to discuss his problem. When we met in the conference room he made it abundantly clear that he wanted Peter removed from the site. I had guessed what was coming and had already decided what my response was going to be. I let him rattle on for about 20 minutes trying to tell me what he considered were all Peter's failures. When he had stopped, I asked him if that was all, to which he replied rather sarcastically "isn't that enough?". I simply told him that I knew Peter better than he ever could and he would be removed over my dead body, got up and walked out.

Things had been building up for some time and it was soon after when I was standing in my office mulling over the many problems, most of which had been inherited from the branch offices, when my phone rang. The stress and pressure of the job had finally got to me as I stood frozen to the spot, not able to pick up the phone. I was shaking all over, with perspiration starting to run down my face. I didn't answer the phone and forced myself to get out of the office. Grabbing my coat, I just left. I got into my car still in a state of distress and found my way to the M23 and drove north. When passing the turn off to Gatwick airport, everything suddenly became clear to me, it was just like a light being switched on in my head. I told myself that I didn't have to live like I was at everyone's beck and call, under so much pressure. Why not walk away and start a new life? I drove on to the end of the motorway, where the M23 meets the M25, and turned around and headed back to Crawley. I went straight to our company secretary and told him of my plan and he undertook to keep it to himself and provide me with all the details of my pension, which he did within a week.

That evening I explained to Jen what I had done and what my plan was. As always she backed me and was pleased I was at last doing something about my situation. Jen was fully aware of the stress I was under. My next move was to tell Graham Baird, our managing director, what I intended to do. He was shocked but shouldn't have been. I told him that I would carry on until the end of the year (1996) – it was June of the same year which would give the firm time to find a replacement.

I had more than work on my mind at this time as Jen had been diagnosed with breast cancer and was undergoing treatment. It wasn't only work that was blowing my mind.

Not long after I had revealed my plans to retire, the Longley family decided to sell the company to a group of investors. When it was all agreed, the new owners approached me to ask if I would consider staying on and they were willing to throw lots of money and perks my way. I knew that if I did not walk away my health would pay a heavy price, one I wasn't prepared to pay. I had known for years that many of Mum's family had suffered from mental illness. I was determined I wouldn't go the same way and never let this happen to me. When I rejected their offer, I was asked if I would leave immediately with a deal that would allow me to draw my salary up until Christmas and keep my company car with the option to buy it at a much reduced price. I was only too pleased to accept the offer which set me free to look after Jen. I left quickly and without any fuss. As soon as I was away I knew I had made the right decision, it was like lifting an enormous weight off of my shoulders.

Jen continued with her treatment following an operation and we gradually got back to some form of normality after some years of struggle. Our minds started to think about what we were going to do with the rest of our lives, apart from gardening and maintaining the house and the thought of having a holiday home, preferably somewhere abroad. We both liked France which we could reach easily from the ferries at Dover and where Jen's brother, Tony, was a director of the ferry line P&O. We started to look in this direction as property prices were low and the exchange rate in favour of the pound was good. We went to a couple of French property exhibitions, but these only had properties that had already been renovated. My idea was to buy a wreck and carry out the work myself. I was still only 55, so more than capable of carrying out the work and I hoped to make some money at the same time. In the end we found several properties on the internet and arranged to view them over several days, but Jen had already made up her mind which one she wanted even before we had looked. It was in a small hamlet in the Limousin called Les Pre.

We decided to visit the area and found a B&B not far from the agent's office whose owners were a couple called Granville and Irene – we should have known better with names like that. We were so caught up in the excitement of everything so didn't give anything a second thought. All the arrangements were made and off we went by car, on the ferry from Dover, down to Paris and then on down through France, travelling time about 10 hours. We managed to find our way to Granville and Irene's so-called B&B. It was a wreck of a place with half completed renovations carried out in the most appalling way. Everywhere I looked I could see mice droppings. It had cheap plastic showers with lukewarm water, I was not impressed. The couple were both very helpful and generous, but it was obvious what they were trying to do was doomed to failure. We were due to stay with them for several days and just could not get out of it, so we stuck it out and roughed it. Rising from our slumber early we got away for the rest of the day to view the properties we had short-listed. The agents turned out to be English and it soon became apparent that we needed to have our wits about us.

After visiting several rundown places we were taken to see the house that Jen had already decided she liked from the internet, and sure enough it was the best of what we had seen. What was on offer was a good-sized house in reasonable condition on the outside and solid, but in poor order, inside. On the ground floor were two bedrooms and a lounge type room where sat a small plastic table with four chairs on which were a multitude of half empty spirit bottles and empty glasses – a locals' meeting place and card school? Up in the large roof space were all sorts of small pieces of farm machinery and piles of grain, all on beautiful terracotta tiles. In the side walls at low level were small window openings to allow the air to circulate and dry the grain. It was obvious that to buy it would mean a great deal of work for us both, but we were looking for a challenge and this was certainly that. It would have to be gutted and rebuilt inside with a completely new layout of the rooms with the construction of bedrooms, bathroom etc. in the roof space. Toilet facilities were non-existent but it did have electricity and water laid on. Outside was a small bake house and about a half-acre of land and a further field of several acres. We thought we could do the majority of the work ourselves and after some negotiation we decided to buy it. Granville had told us he had been a building surveyor in his former life so we thought, wrongly, that he may be useful – he wasn't and it wasn't. After a few days we returned home full of excitement with the task ahead.

We had stayed with Granville and Irene a few times (yes, we did, and I can't think why except that we needed somewhere to sleep and they invited us) and we discovered that someone else was living in the house. All of it was very strange because they never mentioned it, only to say that they had an old lady friend of theirs staying in one of the ground floor rooms off of the kitchen. It was a bit like the situation in Charlotte Bronte's 'Jane Eyre', you heard her but never saw her. It wasn't until much later that we were told she had died and that our couple had inherited all the woman's money. Was she a prisoner and held against her will? We also found out that the woman's family turned up at Grenville and Irene's but were given short-shift and sent on their way, very strange goings on. Everything else relating to the purchase was done by correspondence and then the great day arrived to visit and complete the formalities. We wanted our friends Brian and Brenda to come with us and to be involved with the whole process. We had spent so many years holidaying with them and we valued their opinion and Brian's skill as a draftsman. It was great fun not having to consult anyone else or to answer to others. We settled on a large kitchen, entrance hall and new staircase, lounge and cloakroom and dividing the upstairs into two large bedrooms and a bath/shower room.

The exterior of the house in Les Pre, Limousin.

We arrived at the notaire's office in good time for the signing of the transfer of ownership documents, which Brian and Brenda signed as witnesses. We had done the deed and now owned our own French house. The first priority was to find somewhere to live while carrying out the renovations and re-building work, which is when we had a stroke of luck. Granville had acquired a caravan that was clean, in very good condition and fitted out with everything we needed. Jen and I loved it, except when the water ran out when Jen was halfway through her shower, which seemed to happen with her on a regular basis. Granville suggested we paid him 25 francs a week for the hire, which I thought was reasonable based on 52 weeks a year, but when I came to pay I found that he meant only for the weeks we were using it. I kept quiet and just paid up, a real bargain. He delivered it free of charge and we placed it behind the house and soon connected up the power and water supply, we were in business.

I had noticed when we started work in the mornings some of the insulation materials had been torn and disturbed and suspected rats as we were in a farming area. Consequently, I purchased some poison called 'Ratiside' and we put some of it around the house including inside the external walls. It was the next day when we were sitting with the Bs having our lunch outside the caravan, when we looked up to see a small army of rats appear on the external steps that led up the outside of the house. I am not very brave where rats are concerned but got enough courage together and picked them all up and buried them in the bottom of the field. It wasn't long before Brian and I sealed and filled in all the holes to the house and made good to the complete outside. Anything that wanted to get into the house after that would have had to have bought a pneumatic drill with them.

Both Jen and I worked tirelessly on the house from early morning until late into the evening for 2 to 3 weeks at a time, and then went home to recuperate before returning to carry on where we had left off. We had the whole place rewired and re-plumbed which was carried out by a local tradesman who went by the name of John Pierre. This giant of man worked for the local electrical wholesaler, Monsieur Rodier, who was about half the size of his worker.

I purchased all of the building materials through Granville as he said that he could purchase them cheaper through his trade connections – another mistake on my behalf. I'm convinced he provided me with receipts that showed enhanced prices and made money out of me, I should have known better.

Installing the stairs in our French holiday home in Les Pres, Limousin.

I soon got stuck in, demolishing all the interior partition walls and then had all the exposed timber beams and floor joists grit blasted to remove all the old paint and dirt. They were oak and came up beautifully. When removing a lot of timber boxing in at the front, of what I thought may be a fireplace, I found the most amazing carved stone surround and had this blasted as well to expose a great piece of local craftsmanship. To form the lounge, I managed to scrounge some old oak timbers from Granville and built a half-timbered wall between the hall and the lounge, along which Jen made and hung full length curtains.

Our kitchen was designed to be a traditional French one with large brown ceramic tiles on the floor throughout including the hall and lounge. I started laying the tiles to the kitchen at about 7.30 in the morning and didn't complete it until 10 at night. I would say that it was the most tired I have ever felt in my whole life and believe me I have often been very, very tired. I had to take the next day off to recover. Building the cloakroom on the ground floor was straight forward, it just took time but the installation of the new staircase from the ground floor to the first was something else.

The Bs came down to the house on many occasions to help and it was on one of their visits that Brian and I (mostly Brian) took the dimensions for the manufacture of the staircase, complete with a quarter turned landing. When the time came to fit it, I was on my own with Jen. After assembling the main section all I had to do was to haul it into position on to the bottom quarter landing which had already been fitted by me. I say 'only' as an understatement. The measuring had been critical, if we had been only millimetres out I was sunk. I positioned myself under the stairs and lifted the whole thing onto my back to make the final positioning after tying the top with ropes. One slip, or if the ropes didn't hold, the whole staircase would have come down on top of me. Sounds dramatic but I had tied the ropes properly so I was being very cautious. Fortune and Brian's accuracy in measuring favoured me when the staircase slipped gracefully into exactly the right position with no room to spare.

Building the bedrooms and lining the roof went smoothly with the help of Mathew and his friend Andrew who had been an apprentice when I had been at the old firm. The bath-

Jen and Brian taking a well-earned break from the house renovations in France.

room floor was tiled with new tiles and I used the ones I took up to repair those that were broken in the bedroom areas, which is when I found a Napoleonic coin. I installed new windows throughout the house including the openings used for drying the grain and moved the front door back to its original position. We also engaged contractors to install a new cess pit and drainage system along with major repairs to the roof tiling. The new central heating system was run on liquid gas from a tank installed at the bottom of the garden/field. Finally the whole place was decorated, much of it by Jen with help from Brenda. I had held out against Jen and Brenda's ideas for decorating the kitchen that involved this orange colour for the walls, which I thought would look terrible. They won the day and when completed it looked fantastic.

Once all the work to the house was completed we went about furnishing it in the traditional French style, including a large kitchen table, buffet, traditional sleigh beds and a three-piece suite, plus a number of items that Granville and Irene gave us when they decided to move. It really did turn out amazingly well and we were very pleased. We planted the garden with trees and wild flowers and I built a terrace to finish everything off. When all was over and done, it was time to take it easy on our visits.

It was during one of these times that disaster nearly struck and if it hadn't been for Jen then we would have both perished. In the fireplace to the lounge we decided to install a wood burning stove, one of those tall round ones which look so attractive in different colours – ours was blue. We had a load of logs delivered and to make sure some of them were dried out we stacked a pile on either side of the stove. A few nights later when we were fast asleep in bed Jen shook me and said she could hear noises coming from downstairs. I listened and dismissed the whole thing as I was warm and comfortable and didn't want to move. "Don't worry, just go back to sleep", I said. After a short while she woke me again. I was not a happy man until I put the light on and couldn't see my hand in front of my face, our bedroom was full of smoke. I got out of bed and found my way to the stairs, and on reaching the lounge found that the house was full of smoke with the logs by the stove well alight. I threw open all the windows which started to clear the room sufficiently of smoke, grabbed my gardening gloves and started to throw all the burning logs out of the window onto the terrace outside. Once I had cleared the logs away from the house and made sure that everything was safe and the house free of the smoke we went back to bed.

The moral of this story is always listen to what your wife has to say and don't store logs around a wood burning stove to dry them. There is no doubt in my mind that Jen had saved our lives. Had a spark caught the carpet or the furniture everything would have gone up in flames, including us.

Chapter 13
Moving and Travel

In 1998, Emma introduced us to her new boyfriend, Mike Mooney from New Zealand, who she had met while working in London. Mike worked for an international bank and was also working in London. It was nice for us to meet a boyfriend that we actually liked, so when Emma came home one day and said that Mike had asked her to marry him we were not surprised. On September 10th 1999, Emma and Mike were married at the parish church in Bolney. I won't go into details because that is their story. What I will record is that it was one of the best days of my life, just magical, even allowing for the fact that they were moving to Tokyo.

While all this was going on, Mathew was living a bachelor life in a flat he had bought in Brighton and he just loved it. However, all I could think of was that I had spent all my life trying to get out and away from the place.

We started to use the French house less and less as we had other places to travel to, i.e. Tokyo, and it was obvious to us that Emma would not be returning to England to live and would have no cause to use the house. In the meantime, Mathew was totally immersed in his life in Brighton and we saw less and less of him. We made sure we kept in touch from time to time in the hope that things would change, but they didn't, so we just made sure we were available if he needed us. One thing was certain, he had no interest in holidaying in France and our French house in particular. In the end we made up our minds to sell and use the money for travelling to see the rest of the world before we got too old to do so. We managed to sell and make a reasonable profit for the outlay we had made, but not enough to cover all the hours we had put into it. We had had great fun doing it, it had given us a good experience of living in another country and it had been quite an achievement, so we moved on without any regrets.

Now that Emma and Mathew had moved out, our house in Bolney was large for just the two of us and the upkeep and maintenance was more than we wanted. We were spending more time away holidaying around the world. On April 3rd 2002 our first grandchild, Leo Moses Mooney, was born in Tokyo and we couldn't wait to meet him so within a month of his birth we crept into his room. There he was fast asleep tucked up in the Moses basket that both Emma and Mathew had slept in when they were first born. I whispered in his ear that I was so pleased to meet him, that we would always love him, and he was my favourite boy in all the world. I haven't changed my mind, except we now have further grandsons – Leo, Joshua and Harry – and Jessica our granddaughter who are all very special to Jen and I. We love them and treat them all the same.

After 28 years we decided to move away from Bolney and find a smaller house with less work and easier to lock up and leave, have some neighbours and be nearer to some shops. We searched all over West Sussex with the criteria of three bedrooms, large lounge, kitchen and a smaller garden – not a great deal to ask we thought. We wanted to sell 'Leacroft' as soon as we could so that we had the maximum ready cash available to get the best deal when we found our new home. Our buyer turned out to be a local couple who wanted to be in the village close to her mother. Once sold, we put all our furniture in store and rented a tiny cottage close to the church yard in Cuckfield, the next village to Bolney (it's a small town but property sales are better if estate agents call it a village). Our idea was to sit and wait to see what property would become available as we still hadn't found anywhere we liked, even further away.

One Sunday evening we were travelling back from a visit to the Bs in Findon when we got into a discussion about the kind of property we both liked. When we got as far as the entrance to Cuckfield, and passing through the oldest lower part, Jen pointed out a cottage that she said she really liked the look of and said out of the blue that it was a house she would like to live in. I replied that I preferred one further up the High Street and thought no more of it. On the following Tuesday morning I was on my way to the gym at Burgess Hill and hadn't got far, when in front of me I saw a newly erected 'For Sale' notice outside the very cottage that Jen had said she liked on the previous Sunday evening. I couldn't believe my eyes. Turning the car around in the 'White Harte' pub car park I quickly arrived back at our temporary home. I called up the stairs to Jen that her ideal cottage was up for sale and said we should contact the selling agents, which I did, and made arrangements to view the property 2 hours later at 12.30pm. Jen had something else arranged, so I went on my own to meet the lady of the couple that owned the cottage. They had carried out some alterations to the property, which to my mind were totally inappropriate for the type of property that it was and to a standard I would just not be able to live with, but I could see the potential. After my viewing and a discussion with Jen we decided to make an offer, which was turned down. I didn't think the cottage was worth more than our offer, in fact I thought that our offer was probably more than it was worth, but we were happy to pay to secure the purchase. Before we went any further I wanted Jen to have a look for herself to see what she thought, so we made another arrangement to look together. She loved it and could also see what it could be with our mark stamped on it. We agreed that we wanted the cottage but also that we were not prepared to pay any more than we had already offered so we waited to see if anything else developed. At 6 o'clock that same evening we received a phone call from the husband of the lady I had met earlier in the day who asked if he could come around and see me, which I readily agreed to. When he arrived, we sat down and started to talk about the possible purchase and it was obvious he was keen to do a deal and disclosed that he was desperate to buy another property he had seen – not a sensible admission to a potential buyer. By 6.30pm, the same day, we had come to an agreement and purchased the house at the price we had offered.

Moving to Cuckfield had a number of coincidences, one being that the young couple had called the cottage 'Chateauroux', the name of the nearest town to our house in France where we had purchased the majority of the building materials, furniture, bikes and so much more. All the formalities were completed just when Emma, Mike and Leo had moved to Sydney, Australia, for Mike's job – so we rented the cottage out for 6 months and went to stay near them. Sydney to me is one of the greatest cities on the planet, we loved it and stayed there on many extended trips.

On our return to Cuckfield we set about completely stripping out all of the work that the previous couple had done so that we could recreate the house to reflect its age of somewhere around the mid 18th century. We moved doorways, stripped out ceilings to expose the original oak joists, replaced all the ground floor doors with solid oak ones, laid oak floors, installed a period fireplace, raised the ceiling in the kitchen and replaced all the kitchen units and laid ceramic floor tiles – all topped off with a complete electrical rewire and plumbing and heating system. When finished and fitted out with some of our old furniture and rugs it had been transformed to reflect the age of the house and we were very pleased with the result.

Back in the 1800s we found that our new purchase had been two farm workers cottages and then became a general store and candle makers owned by a Mr Bristy, following which it became the village laundry. We renamed the house 'Old Laundry'.

During the time we were working on the house I decided to take up the floor to the third bedroom, as parts of it had been replaced with poor materials and even worse workmanship. On removing the floor, I found that spaces between the floor joists were packed tightly with brazil nut shells, the reason for which I couldn't fathom out. I remembered that when my old firm were carrying out renovation works at 'Hampton Court' palace they had discovered that seashells had been used to deaden the sound between the floor joists, but this seemed a little far-fetched for our old cottage. I looked at the shells more closely and then the penny dropped, I could see little teeth marks in the sides of the shells, rats I thought. The rats had taken the shells from the general store below and broken them open to eat the kernels and then used the shells to build their nests.

I cleared them all out before laying the new floor and while I was doing so found a George IV penny, just like I had found the Napoleonic one in the floor at the French house – another coincidence.

Jen remodelled the garden to include an area to grow vegetables and completely trans-formed it while I built a new sunken patio and steps to finish everything off.

It was during the work on the cottage that Mathew turned up with his new girlfriend, Sam Stern. I was covered in paint and filler and not looking at my best, I didn't know they were coming. I liked our future daughter-in-law from the beginning and she quickly became one of our family. At last, Mathew had found the right person to marry – which they did on May 23rd 2008. The wedding was such fun for everyone with lots of traditional Jewish involvement including the band during the evening. I danced with anyone and everyone all in the authentic way. My brothers were convinced that I had been taking lessons, but it all just came naturally. We now have a further two young grandsons, Joshua and Harry, quite a handful but we love them.

With a smaller house and garden, I now had more time to do other things. Jen fixed me up with golf lessons, which I had never played before, I went back to my efforts at water colour painting and we both joined a volunteer organisation at Shoreham called 'Coast Watch' as lookouts for shipping and the general public should they experience difficulties at sea.

During this time, I became heavily involved with the Cuckfield museum and joined the committee carrying out and supervising any maintenance work, amongst other duties. One of the highlights for me was my development into becoming the museum's guide by taking different groups of visitors on historical walks around the town and explaining its past. This is something I still do and thoroughly enjoy, including meeting and getting to know so many different people.

I continued to research my family tree which I had neglected for many years. It was while working on the family tree that I sent off for a copy of my great grandfather and grandmother's wedding certificate, only to find that they had been married in the parish church in Cuck-field where we had just moved to and could see the spire from our lounge window. I made

Family Christmas in New Zealand, 2018.

contact with the church secretary and she informed me that they still had a copy of all the original records and that I could go and have a look at them. I found them in an old cupboard tucked away in a corner of the church and went through them. I dis-covered the original entry of the marriage in 1841 of William Constable and Jane Lywood, my great great grandparents. It then came to me that there may be oth-ers, so I started looking further back and to my astonishment I found the entry for my great, great, great grandparents, Edward and Ann Constable, who had died in the local workhouse in 1779 and 1805 respectively and were buried in the churchyard. I have been able to identify the position where they are buried with the help of the wife of the grave digger, Dick, who works for the local undertaker Pat Gallagher – the very same Pat Gallagher who was Mathew's football coach years before.

I have so many questions I would love to ask my ancestors, ones that I am sure I shall never know the answers too. Are all these things a coincidence?

Chapter 14
Travelling

The years have passed all too quickly, and we now spend the winters in New Zealand where Emma, Mike, Leo and Jessica live. The thought of not seeing our grandchildren grow up without knowing us was too much, so we decided very early on that we would spend as much time with them as possible. The places that we have spent with them have included Tokyo, Singapore, Australia and now New Zealand.

It was on one of our early trips to New Zealand that Jen decided, and I agreed (I don't know why for the life of me), to go on a sailing course. Jen had already been sailing on and off for years with her Dad – I had not. We were put through our paces over 3 days and then considered to be sufficiently proficient to receive our certificates of competence. We were now due to go off on our own for a few days and were pointed in the right direction. Before leaving, our instructor informed us that the 'TAIL END' of a cyclone was expected to pass through but if we turned east at the mouth of the river where it meets the sea, 'we should be able to make it' to a cove on a particular island in time to shelter. We managed to get to the river estuary, turned right and looked behind us and saw black clouds gathering. In about 2 hours we found the island and sailed into the sheltered cove, the only problem was that every other boat in a radius of many miles had arrived and were already anchored up before us. We managed to find a spot out of the prevailing wind and got the anchor down. We were very proud and relieved that we had made it. After having something to eat, the wind got stronger and settling down for the night we could hear the wind getting up even more. At about 2 o'clock in the morning we could hear voices above the raging winds and just laid there listening. The boat was rocking and rolling all over the place and the voices got louder. I decided, with Jen's encouragement, to go outside and see what all the noise was about. At the stern of our vessel stood two men hanging on for dear life looking down into the water where there was a third man fully dressed with a rope in his hand. I wondered what I needed to do, being buffeted about, and could only just hang on. I managed to get to where the men were standing to question them to see what they were up to. The wind was howling, the rough sea was throwing me from side to side while the other boat was bouncing off of our small craft – and it was obvious to me that the men had been drinking. What I could make out was that my drunken sailors had decided to move their yacht from the other side of the bay to a more protected position alongside us and their anchor rope had got entwined around our anchor, dragging us both towards the rocks. As the man in the water was fully clothed I was concerned for his safety, but he just kept diving down into the water in an effort to free his rope. I was starting to get very worried and was considering trying to get ashore to the island when a shout went up that the rope had been freed. Our problem now was that our anchor was now free, and our boat was being dashed against the rocks which we had suddenly got very close to. With the help of one of the other men we got the motor started and got ourselves away and out into clear water and our anchor down. Then the man who had come with us just said that he was off to find his boat and just dived into the swirling sea – we were horrified.

The following morning, we could see the other boat parked up in the same spot it had left the night before to seek better shelter and that had caused all the problems. All three men were on deck when a woman appeared in her bikini, put on her sun cream, and gently dived in for a swim. We could see the funny side and presumed she had stayed in bed throughout all the drama of the night before.

We had just decided that we would return the way we had come, and get rid of the boat, when an older man arrived alongside in his kayak to check that we were OK. He told us that he and his wife could see we were in trouble during the night and had stayed awake to watch over us in case we needed rescuing. Once we had assured him that we were fine he invited us to lunch on his luxury motor launch. It was a floating gin palace – much more to my idea of life at sea. Once we had had the grand tour of the boat we were invited to sit down on the back deck under the shade to enjoy a slap-up lunch. I decided then and there that if I ever went to sea again it would be in a vessel just like the one we were on. Since our experience I have managed to avoid going on, or in, the sea and have no intentions of doing so.

We have also had trips on our own to many other parts of the world including Jordan which left an everlasting memory of a very bleak experience. Jen had, for a long time, wanted to visit the historical lost city of Petra and other sites and I became keen to go. All was well when we slept under canvas, went river walking, and saw Petra by day and by night to see the treasury lit up by candle light. The evening before we were due to leave to visit T. E. Lawrence's house, and then the Dead Sea, all was well when we went to bed at our hotel. I got up in the early hours of the morning to visit the bathroom. I was washing my hands and looking in the mirror was the last thing I remember until I came around laying over the side of the bath. I knew straight away that I had seriously injured my left leg. I dragged myself back to my bed and found Jen awake and explained what had happened. I laid as still as I could, but I was in a lot of pain. We waited as long as we could before contacting our tour leader, who straight away made contact with the hotel staff and they contacted the emergency services. I was carted off to a military hospital and dumped into what I can only describe as a cell, complete with metal bars in the door and at the small window. While waiting for a doctor to see me I was visited by some very strange people who just stood by my bed looking at me, I concluded that I was probably in a mental hospital. When the so-called doctor arrived he insisted that if I was able to lay still for a few weeks the whole problem would resolve itself. In time it was decided that perhaps I should have some X-rays taken. When they did, I remember the sound I was making while drifting in and out of consciousness from the pain they were causing me trying to lift me into position on the machine. The hospital would not give me any pain killers until we had paid cash for them. The problem was we had very little, certainly not as much as the hospital's demands. After Jen had contacted the tour operator's representative, arrangements were made for a taxi driver to pick up a bundle of cash who then delivered it to Jen. The pain relief when it came was not that great, but it helped.

It took several days to sort out the numerous red tape surrounding the travel insurance, including a period when the insurance company tried to infer we were not covered adding more unnecessary stress. When everything was resolved, we were told that I was to be transferred to the capital Amman to the private Red Crescent hospital.

The day for us to leave couldn't come quick enough. Trying to get the stretcher with me on it into the ambulance was a whole episode on its own. I was pushed and shoved into the ambulance a dozen times while the driver, and a pretend doctor, attempted to get the wheels engaged with the track on which the stretcher should have run. Eventually they managed to get the two wheels nearest my head to engage but not the ones nearest my feet, so they left that end loose. It soon became apparent that the pretend doctor was not going to lower himself, so Jen had to sit at my feet with her feet on the bottom of the stretcher in an attempt to stop it jumping all over the place. We had approximately 200 miles to travel on the most appalling roads full of pot holes and other drivers trying to dodge them. After we had been travelling for about an hour, Jen started to feel travel sick so she had to move to the front of the vehicle next to the driver. I was left to fend for myself after the other attendant had given up making himself more comfortable and secure. I don't remember much about the journey, only the odd bit when I was conscious. We travelled on mile after mile, nothing to drink and no attention to my plight.

When we eventually arrived at the hospital everything changed. Several staff were waiting to receive me including the hospital's orthopaedic surgeon, who was to prove to be my saviour. I was immediately given proper pain relief and put in a private room, the transformation in my care was amazing. Arrangements had been made for Jen to stay at a new top hotel some distance from the hospital which gave me something else to worry about as I was concerned for her safety. I should have known better, she had taxis arranged morning and night to get to and fro to see me and she made sure she phoned me when she got back to her room in the evening.

After a broken night's sleep, I was visited by the surgeon who had met me the day before. He introduced himself as Dr Sammy and informed me that I would be having a scan and further X-rays. My heart sank on this news as any movement of my leg sent unbelievable pain throughout my whole body, I wasn't sure I could go through it all over again. Dr Sammy was very reassuring – I wasn't so sure. Even writing this is making me feel quite ill. When the team of orderlies came for me I insisted and lectured them on how everything had to be co-ordinated so that I went up and down in one easy motion. What they thought of the mad Englishman I simply don't know. It took six of them to lift me on to the machine, which they did as smoothly as they could – even then I passed out. Once all the pictures had been taken, Dr Sammy came to see me again and told me that he had found a break in my femur close to my hip joint. He went on to say that I needed an operation to pin my leg as early as possible. All I could think of was that I wanted to get home to be treated by our own NHS, what if I was given contaminated blood? Did this man have any idea what he wanted to do to me? Dr Sammy was so kind and understanding and explained in plain language why it was so important to get my leg fixed quickly and even gave me his word that he would take personal care of me. Once we got talking it turned out that he had been trained in the UK and that one of his assignments had been in our local NHS hospital. An even bigger coincidence was that he had trained with the surgeon who had fixed my arm all those years before and had known him well.

I had the operation which entailed inserting metal rods (he called them pins) up through my leg from the inside of my knee which were then screwed into the top section of my femur. I spent the next 3 weeks getting myself fit enough to travel home. This sounds easier now than it was, I was in a state of shock from what I had been through. Every time the staff tried to get me out of bed I would faint.

Jen arrived one day when I was laying prostrate on a leaned back chair, she said afterwards that my skin was white and transparent. It is the only time throughout my ordeal that I thought I was going to die and that I wouldn't get home. In time I recovered sufficiently enough to allow Dr Sammy to let me travel, he even cancelled his family holiday to stay with me until it was time for me to leave. The day before we were due to fly home he turned up with a wheelchair and pushed me up on to the roof terrace and pointed out all the places of interest in Amman city.

When the day arrived for me to leave all the staff who had looked after me, and been so generous and kind, were there to see me off. Dr Sammy made sure I had everything I needed: crutches, large zimmer frame to fit my height, and more importantly an express way through customs. We said our goodbyes, I had been so lucky to have met Dr Sammy a truly wonderful man. I was already thinking of a return trip in the future to meet up when I could thank everyone again and they could see the end results of all their attention and kindness.

Once home I started to improve but it took a long time to fully recover, much more than I ever imagined it would. I was so pleased to be home. After a few weeks I felt well enough to want to email Dr Sammy to express my thanks and to update him on how I was progressing. I had also made contact through a friend with the surgeon who Dr Sammy had trained with at our local hospital and he had asked to be put in touch him. As I didn't have an address for Dr Sammy I emailed the hospital and asked them if they could let me have it. I sent the email and waited. After a few days I got a reply from the administrator at the hospital which simply said, "Thank you for your email, I am sorry to inform you that 3 days after you were discharged from Dr Sammy's care he collapsed and died of a heart attack. I hope you are progressing well". I was completely shocked and filled with sadness, I owed this man so much and now he was gone. A truly great man lost to Jordan and the world of medicine.

Many of my work colleagues, especially the ones that were so close to me, have now joined the great construction company in the sky. Just before my retirement I was informed that Curly had been diagnosed with cancer – smoking as much as he did must have contributed I'm sure. I went to see him at home and took him a bottle of his favourite whisky. Knocking on his door I could hear puffing and blowing coming along the hallway. When he opened the door, I was quite shocked to see how he had deteriorated in such a short time. I was greeted in his usual manner, "Oh, you have decided to come to see me have you, thought you were never coming!". I had only been with him 3 weeks earlier. We chatted for quite a while before I left, he looked very tired. It was the last time I saw him as he was gone within a short time after.

I had seen Peter Weeks from time to time when I had dropped in to his sites in various places but hadn't seen him for a bit when I got the message that he had been taken seriously ill with cancer. John Ebdon and I went to visit him at the Royal Marsden Hospital in a specialist cancer unit. When we entered his room I could see that he was gravely ill but, like the Peter of old, he was full of enthusiasm and very optimistic about the future. I visited several times on my own including when he was sent home to be cared for. Emma came home for one summer and he was keen to meet up with her, so I arranged for him to come to our new house in Cuckfield.

It was during one of my visits to see him he suddenly went very quiet and then recalled right out of the blue an incident that I had forgotten all about. He went on to say, "Richard, I have always admired and respected you for your fairness and your honesty". I didn't know what to say. "Oh, why's that then Pete?", I replied. "Do you remember the time when I had made a big error and used the wrong strength concrete on the job I was managing?". As it happened I had forgotten all about the problem and even the outcome. He went on to remind me that I had been summoned to a meeting in London with the client, architects, engineers and quantity surveyors. It would seem that I had told Peter to dress in his best suit and to look the smartest and tidiest he possibly could, I was taking him with me. When we got to the meeting everyone ganged up against us, and Peter in particular. He went on to say that I wasn't having any of it and defended him and the firm against all comers even though he had made the error. He even said that he had begun to doubt that he had been in the wrong! "After the meeting" he said, "we walked down the road together and stood on the corner of the street, where you gave me the biggest bollocking I have ever had, but you had stood by me and I have never forgotten." I sat there stunned, he had remembered all those years and had never let me down. I went to visit Peter for the last time at his home in Crawley when he was propped up on his pillows in a cot-like bed. I sat and held his hand, talking to him about the time we had worked together. He couldn't answer and just squeezed my hand in recognition, I found it very distressing. Another one of my friends and colleagues died a few days later.

John Ebdon, following his retirement, had kept busy working for the Church of England administering all the construction work on the churches in the Diocese of Chichester. In about 2014, I was contacted and told that he had been taken ill, suffering from a heart attack. I went to visit him, and he seemed to recover reasonably well. Some time later, I was again contacted and told that John had been admitted to St Catherine's Hospice in Crawley which he had founded and had spent many years as Chairman of the governing board. I went to see him and found Janet, his wife, sitting beside him. She told me afterwards that she could see the shock on my face as I walked in the room, I hardly recognised him. He sadly died soon after.

All three of my closest friends and colleagues had gone to that great construction site in the sky, a very sobering thought.

Chapter 15
The Future

What the future holds of course I don't know but being a person who has always had an opinion on most things I do have my ideas on things to come.

Based on the progress and changes which have occurred during my life I see a great future for our planet, if we don't destroy it first. My main prediction is to forecast the discovery of new forms of life on other planets. How anyone can think that in the vastness of space that humans, or their like, are on their own is simply ridiculous to my mind.

In the immediate future we will have some form of flying personal vehicles, based on the car principle. Space travel will continue to many other planets and with any luck humans will decide to put their differences to one side and work together for the goodness of mankind. From my building construction perspective, I always said to our staff that when someone invents a computer that can lay bricks and put roofs on buildings then I would be the first to get one. They have just invented one. Poverty will be made a thing of the past and the scourge of human pollution of our world will be defeated. Ways of storing electric power will be invented so that human survival will be assisted by natural power generation, this is already underway.

I truly believe that I have lived through a wonderful period of history but also think that the best years are yet to come. If only I could be here to witness it.

If it is at all possible to watch the future unfold, and keep a watching eye over my children, grandchildren and future generations and my family to come, then you can rest assured I will be doing just that.

Mathew, Sam, Joshua and Harry now live a short distance away from us in Henfield, and we are able to see them for the greater part of the year, but as the winters seem to get colder Jen and I now spend them in New Zealand. We stay close to Emma, Mike, Leo and Jessica and this is where I have written this account of my life. I'm not sure if future generations will find it of interest – I hope they do, but if not I have thoroughly enjoyed remembering and thinking how lucky I have been.

Most of what I have written about has set down the events and stories of my life. Like most people of my generation, I have experienced highs and lows. At times it has been a struggle, but I would not have wished to have lived my life at a different time in history. I have had all the benefits of modern society with the advancement of medicine and travel, electricity, central heating, computers, cars, planes, mobile phones, and on and on. My family, and my generation in general, also experienced the very harsh times which followed the Second World War with all its deprivations, poverty and austerity. Therefore, we can appreciate our good fortune from what it was to what it is today.

Most of what I have achieved, if anything, has been down to hard work and good fortune, although I do wonder what I could have done if a better education had been available to me when I was young. On the other hand, I probably wouldn't have had the experiences I have had and not have a balanced view on the world as a whole.

This is my story, a tale teller's tale, shaped by those who have always been closest to me: my family and friends.